Norway 1940
The Forgotten Fiasco

Norway 1940

The Forgotten Fiasco

Joseph Kynoch

Airlife

Copyright © 2002 Joseph Kynoch

First published in the UK in 2002
by Airlife Publishing Ltd

British Library Cataloguing-in-Publication Data
A catalogue record for this book is available from the British Library

ISBN 1 84037 380 6

Typeset by Phoenix Typesetting, Burley-in-Wharfedale, West Yorkshire
Printed in England by MPG Books Ltd., Bodmin, Cornwall

For a complete list of all Airlife titles please contact:

Airlife Publishing Ltd
101 Longden Road, Shrewsbury, SY3 9EB, England
E-mail: sales@airlifebooks.com
Website: www.airlifebooks.com

DEDICATION

To the memory of my comrades of the North West Expeditionary Force and our Norwegian Allies, with whom we fought, side by side for the freedom of Norway in April 1940, and especially those who died in the cause of freedom and now rest in peace in the beautiful valley of the Gudbrandsdalen and the little villages and towns of Norway.

The characters in this book are real people and were my comrades in Norway 1940, and a few still are. The events related in this book actually happened and although some of the words used may not have been the same, they are similar in all respects.

Acknowledgements

Without the help of some of my veteran comrades of 146 and 148 Brigades, I would have found it difficult to put this book together.

Their memories and photographs of those far-off days, some of which I have been able to incorporate in this book, brought back to my own memory the terrors and anxieties which we faced in that unhappy land of Norway in early 1940.

To mention them all here by name would be superfluous but one or two supplied me with information that I would not otherwise have obtained, like W/T Jack Briggs of the Royal Navy whose job it was to set up a radio station at Aandalsnes, our base and Colonel E.C.G. Beckwith's unpublished diary of the Sherwood Foresters' action in Norway as far as Tretten Gorge.

My thanks are also due to the Imperial War Museum for their valued assistance with recordings made by my comrades.

CONTENTS

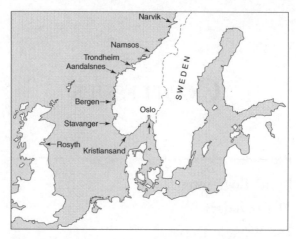

Map 1a   The British Isles and Western Europe.

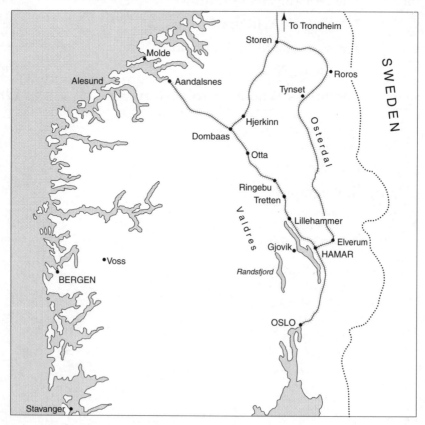

Map 1b   The Norwegian rail system.

PROLOGUE

Over half a century has passed by since April 1940 and the utter chaos that was dubbed the North West Expeditionary Force and sent on its way to the frozen land of Norway, the land of the midnight sun, to free it from the Nazi invaders.

Chaos not only reigned throughout the preparation for the British Forces to leave the shores of the UK but also followed in the footsteps of the expedition to the shores of Norway. There even more chaos followed the brave young men, lads mostly in their teens and early twenties, into the jaws of an enemy already 'blooded' on the plains of Poland.

For myself and a lot of my comrades of the 1/5th Leicesters, it was confusion almost from the beginning of our call-up which continued long after we boarded the two coasters the *St Magnus* and the *St Sunniva*, that were to take us some 500 miles across the North Sea to meet the enemy. But it was all too late and something akin to stemming a flood with a yard broom.

There's not many of us left now who can tell the story of the battles which raged fiercely but briefly for ten days or so in a far-off valley in central Norway, just south of the Arctic Circle.

The German Army Group Pellengahr had already established itself in the south of the country in the western coastal towns and Trondheim in the north. It was armed to the teeth with all the most modern aircraft and weaponry of war. When our 148 Brigade landed at Molde (Map 1b) about 8 p.m. on 18 April, the Germans were already marching north to meet us as they pushed the Norwegian army backwards.

148 Brigade was the first unit of the British army to make contact with the German army in the Second World War, but for some reason we never achieved our full complement of three battalions and were almost a thousand men short. We were given the fearsome code name of Operation Sickleforce. All that was left of these two poorly trained battalions – the 1/5th Leicesters, which was my own battalion, and the 1/8th Sherwood Foresters, almost two thousand men, were some three officers and about one hundred and sixty other ranks when we were taken aboard the cruisers *Sheffield* and *Galatea*. They rescued us from the smoking ruins of the town of Aandalsnes in the early hours of the morning of 2 May

1940. This was the first evacuation of our troops from the European mainland and, somehow, we knew there would be others.

Some of the more terrifying moments stand out in my memory so clearly that they could have happened yesterday. The way we described it on the way back home across 500 miles of hostile sea was 'If it hadn't been so frightening, it would have been laughable.'

This was indeed the First Dunkirk but although we didn't know when it would happen, we knew the BEF in France would suffer the same fate as ourselves but on a much larger scale. We now knew the meaning of the word 'Blitzkrieg'. We had experienced it.

Cruiser HMS *Sheffield.*

Norway 1940
The Forgotten Fiasco

ONE

IN THE BEGINNING

T he war began for me and most of my comrades of the 2/5th
Battalion of the Leicestershire Regiment, on Monday 28 August
1939, after our annual summer camp; which, for that year was on
Holyhead Island in North Wales.

The buff envelope with the letters OHMS on it dropped through the
letterbox at home. It ordered me to report at the TA centre in Ulverscroft
Road on 1 September, and it was on that very day that the German army
crossed the border into Poland.

We knew then that Britain would have to declare war on Germany
along with her ally France and that this would be the beginning of the
Second World War and the end of our personal freedom as we had
known it. From now on, we would have no choice but to obey orders
which would be given from above, starting with those of a lance corporal.
I remember that sunny Sunday morning, 3 September, when we
marched as a battalion with bayonets fixed, through the centre of the city

Staindrop village, County Durham.

1

of Leicester. We were watched by cheering crowds of people and with the regimental band playing 'It's a long way to Tipperary' at the head of the column on our way to church. I felt very proud at that moment to be in the Leicesters.

At eleven o'clock the service was interrupted by the Prime Minister's voice on the wireless in the church, telling us that the ultimatum which Britain had given to Hitler to withdraw his troops from Poland by 11 a.m. otherwise a state of war would exist between Germany and Britain and France, had expired and no reply had been received, consequently we were now at war with Germany. There was a noticeable hush in the church after this announcement, and quite a few grim faces.

The battalion was quickly organised and HQ Company, to which I belonged, was put into billets in Havelock Street in Leicester and we were paid the nominal sum of ten shillings a week, or fifty pence in today's money, whilst we were there. With cigarettes at one shilling, or five new pence, for twenty and beer at five new pence for two pints, we didn't do so bad but we didn't have any change left in our pockets by the next pay day; especially if we had been home on weekend pass or to a local cinema to see the latest film.

Most of us smoked in those days, mainly because we didn't have much to do in the early days of mobilisation but draw extra equipment and attend the local gas chamber to test our new respirators. We very soon got through twenty cigarettes each day; also, we discovered fairly quickly that if we couldn't afford to drink beer, then we had to drink cider at just about half the price and it was really potent.

It was because of drinking this brew with my mates in the local that I became ill in the billet one night and was put on a charge by the orderly corporal and had to do my very first spell of 'jankers' the following day peeling potatoes in the cookhouse.

During those early days we always seemed to be on parade for something, and if it wasn't for drawing kit it would almost certainly be for an update of injections or perhaps it would be a dental parade.

After a few weeks we saw on daily orders one morning that some of us had been transferred to the 1/5 Battalion based in Loughborough and this for me was just the job, for my home was in the village of Thorpe Acre on the outskirts of the town and with a bit of luck I might be able to sleep there. Unfortunately, this situation didn't last long and shortly afterwards we saw on daily orders that some of us had been posted to Derby to guard the Rolls-Royce factory there. Myself and both my mates 'Taffy' Jones and Arthur Ridgeway were included in the posting, which made it more acceptable, even something of an adventure. After a few days and nights of routine guard duty, two hours on and four hours off all through the day and night, the novelty soon began to wear off and we all felt as though one good undisturbed night of sleep was badly needed.

The Loughborough contingent, 1/5 Leicesters. Back row from left: Platoon Serg/Major Gilbert, PTE G. Burnham, PTE Needham, PTE Dormer, PTE R. Coleman, PTE G. Glenn, PTE 'Squeek' Adams, PTE J. Kynoch, PTE G. Williams, PTE Bryant, PTE Bob Holt, PTE Monk.   Middle row from left: CQMS 'Paddy' Simpson, PTE Clapton, PTE Wilson, PTE Veasey, PTE Lee, PTE Wooton, PTE Kelham, PTE Wooton, PTE Gough, Corp. W.A. Thomas, PTE R. Sutton, PTE S. Newby.   Front row from left: LT. Sid Morson, (Battn QM) Captain Hobbins, Mrs Dean, Mayor George Dean, Colonel Toller, Major John German, RQMS Halford, Standing Stan Pollard PTE.

The local kids used to come and watch us mount guard outside the main gates of the factory and then they would tag on behind us as we marched up and down outside, more often than not, getting in the way as we patrolled back and forth along the street.

After a week or so of this, we were moved back to the battalion and one dark frosty night, we boarded a train with our haversack rations of bread and cheese and moved north to the sleepy little village of Staindrop in the county of Durham.

Here HQ Company was stationed in the grounds of Raby Castle, the remainder of the battalion being stationed at the nearby villages of Cockfield, Evenwood and Bishops Auckland. It was here that I discovered that I had been put in the MT platoon, who were billeted in the stable buildings some little way across the park from the castle. Our billets were just above the stables in a draughty old loft which had a cold concrete floor, access to which was up a well-worn flight of stone steps attached to the outside wall of the building. Here, in this group of buildings were also located the company office, the guard room and CQMS Paddy Simpson's stores.

We slept on beds which consisted of three planks of wood which rested on two wooden cross-pieces, one at the head of the bed and the other at the foot, which raised the planks about six inches above the concrete floor. Onto these planks we put our straw-filled palliasses and pillows and covered ourselves with the regulation issue of three blankets and on top of this I spread my greatcoat for extra warmth.

These sleeping arrangements were just the job for the orderly corporal, who was almost sure to be Fred 'Po' Chambers, shortly afterwards made up to Transport Sergeant. He seemed to take a sadistic delight in kicking away the cross-pieces from under our beds at reveille and unfortunately for me, my bed was the first one in from the doorway. He was a big chap, was Po, and would probably have turned the scales to fifteen stone although he was only about five foot eight or so and in his early thirties. He had a round chubby face with humorous lines which he tried to cover up under scowls and his bald head added to the impossibility of his trying to look stern to us raw recruits.

Soon after we had arrived in Durham, I discovered that I had been posted on detached duty to divisional HQ at Bedale Hall with just about the only fifteen hundredweight truck in the battalion, with instructions to report to the RQMS there. For several weeks I drove him about Yorkshire between various military establishments scattered about between Catterick, Northallerton and that beautiful old town of Richmond, with its cobbled square, and finally to Malton, where my detached duty came to an end. A week or so before Christmas I was back in Staindrop to be met with rumours that we were bound for Finland, where the Russians had invaded at the end of November. Now I discovered that I was no longer in the MT platoon but with the Bren carriers under 2nd Lieutenant A.B. Speak (Speak and I shall hear). The platoon was billeted in the village hall in the main street that had been somewhat modified to accommodate some thirty men. Heat was provided by the usual coke stove in the centre of the room. I wasn't very pleased with this changeover for there was still only one Bren carrier available so our time was mainly taken up with map reading and stripping and reassembling our one and only Bren gun, with competitions to see who could do it the fastest.

The platoon was crowded into the hall with just about a foot between each bed.

I was not back very long before I picked up a 'flu germ and woke up one morning with a very high temperature and raving about all sorts of things in a kind of semi-delirium, just in time to see a young chap from across the other side of the room being taken out on a stretcher, which put the wind up me so much that I fainted. Afterwards, I learned that the poor chap had contracted meningitis and had died. We were all very quickly removed from the hall and put into isolation for about two weeks in a wooden hut somewhere on the estate.

This particular time was what the Americans called the 'phoney' war, simply because nothing very much was happening on the Western Front in France, where the British Expeditionary Force was preparing with the French to meet any sudden onslaught by the Germans. But this period was not so 'phoney' as the Americans made it out to be, for preliminary skirmishes began to take place between the British and German navies.

Early in December the papers were full of reports about an enemy battleship operating in the Indian Ocean and the South Atlantic, leaving a trail of sinkings of British ships of the merchant fleet in its wake which amounted to a tonnage of some 50,000, all carrying valuable cargoes which the British could ill afford to lose.

The aircraft carrier *Ark Royal* had scoured the southern seas with her escorts in an effort to come to grips with the raider, but without success.

By mid-December, there came a story in the papers that the pride of the German navy, the pocket battleship *Admiral Graf Spee*, which had been responsible for all the sinkings in the southern oceans, had been damaged in action with the British cruisers *Exeter*, *Achilles* and *Ajax* off the coast of South America and had put into Montevideo harbour for repairs. She was eventually scuttled in the River Plate.

Christmas came and most of us went on leave to our various homes in the towns and villages of Leicestershire, pleased to get away for a short while from the cold, wintry moors of Durham and back to the more familiar surroundings of our homes and families. We somehow felt that this would be our last leave before we became actively involved in another world war and we all began to wonder anxiously where we would be sent to on active service.

Early in the New Year of 1940 we found ourselves once more back in our various billets in Staindrop and Raby Castle. We had not been back from leave very long before I found myself covered with the spots of German measles and back in isolation with one or two others in a large house in the main street of the village.

By the end of the month rumours were rife in the battalion that we were very shortly going to be sent overseas to help the hard-pressed Finns, who were putting up such a good fight to keep the invading Russians out of their country.

At this time, the whole world was watching the action of the brave Finns, whose appeals for volunteers and arms to assist their small army caused a prolonged diplomatic wrangle when Norway and Sweden both refused the passage of Allied troops across their territories. Even though, as members of the League of Nations, they were more or less obliged to let Allied troops go to the defence of Finland, who was also a member state. The trouble was they were afraid of jeopardising their neutrality if seen to be helping their frail little neighbour who was more than a match for the Russian hordes.

So, on 5 February, the supreme War Council of the League of Nations approved a British scheme, Plan 4, for the provision of two or more Allied brigades on the Finnish front which were timed to go into action by mid-March. The brigades were to be landed at Narvik to block German efforts to obtain the valuable iron ore required for their armament factories. But the two brigades, one of which was our own 148, didn't move, for on 12 March, while their guns were active on all fronts, a peace treaty was signed between Finland and Russia. Then on 15 March an interesting development in the Norwegian situation and the course of the war came about. A British reconnaissance plane which had been patrolling the 'leads' (small islands off the coast of Norway) spotted what was thought to be the much sought after *Altmark*, the German auxiliary ship, entering the Jossing Fjord, south of Stavanger (Map 2). As she reached the shelter of the fjord, she was closely shadowed by two British destroyers, HMS *Intrepid* and HMS *Cossack,* along with two Norwegian torpedo boats.

Captain Dau was the German skipper of the *Altmark,* which had plenty of cargo space beneath the hatches and in the holds below; where British prisoners from the many victims of the *Graf Spee* had lived for many months in complete darkness. Some even had to use a filthy stinking oil tank for living space. The food was nauseating and insufficient and many of them were suffering from scurvy. For days on end, they were kept below decks and never allowed up for fresh air or exercise.

Captain Vian of *Cossack* challenged the Norwegian torpedo boats and said he had good reason to believe that British prisoners were being held aboard the *Altmark* and suggested that the ship should be conducted to Bergen and searched. The Norwegians refused and said that the ship had already been searched at Bergen and had been granted permission to proceed.

This was not true, but the destroyer nevertheless withdrew and Captain Vian got in touch with Whitehall by radio. After giving his report, he was told to go back into the fjord forthwith and release the British prisoners from the *Altmark.*

The Norwegians were again given the opportunity by Captain Vian to help in a friendly way but they refused, and so after dark *Cossack* steamed back into the fjord and what happened then was told in two-inch head-lines in British and European newspapers.

Captain Dau of the *Altmark* tried to ram *Cossack* as she approached, but failed. He then tried to blind the *Cossack* by training his searchlight on the

Map 2   Norway's coastal towns.

bridge, but again failed and the destroyer pulled alongside the freighter.

A boarding party of twenty ratings from *Cossack* quickly overwhelmed the guards and yelled down through the hatches 'The Navy's here, lads.'

That night almost three hundred seamen of the mercantile marine were on their way home to Britain.

The Norwegians immediately protested against what they called 'This gross violation of our territorial waters which has aroused strong indignation.' Not satisfied with a mere protest, the Norwegians demanded that the British prisoners, taken at gunpoint from the German ship, be handed over to the Norwegian Government and damages paid.

No wonder Winston Churchill said afterwards in the House 'What kind of people do they think we are?'

M. Hambro, President of the Norwegian Parliament, stated that it was 'an insolent and impetuous intrusion on the sovereign rights of this small country which by tradition is the best friend of England.' Cassandra of the *Daily Mirror*, stated quite boldly in his column, 'If these are the actions of a friend, who needs enemies?'

The German minister at Oslo complained that it was an unheard of violation of international law and even accused Norway of not giving sufficient protection to the prison ship.

Professor Koht, the Norwegian Foreign Minister, said that their authorities were unaware that British prisoners were held on the *Altmark*, but Neville Chamberlain, our Prime Minister, replied to this in the House by saying that:

> Considering that the fact was published in newspapers throughout the world, I can only regard this as a surprising statement. According to Professor Koht, the Norwegian Government see no objection to the use of their territorial waters for hundreds of miles by a German transport ship for the purpose of escaping capture on the high seas and of conveying British prisoners to a German prison camp. Such a policy for a neutral country is at variance with international law as the British Government understand it and the abuse of neutral waters by German warships is unacceptable.

So the controversy went on in the papers which kept us all fully up to date with the situation. We read them eagerly and this particular episode made a good many of us wonder what kind of people the Norwegians were. Little did we realise at the time that very soon we would find out for ourselves.

By the beginning of April we knew that things were moving at last and that Hitler's plans to invade Scandinavia were very close to activation. Before the month was more than three days old, the Leicesters and Foresters were packing their kit and by 6 April we were on the move.

Two

The Invaders

We very quickly discovered that the plans made by the powers in control of our destinies and the prosecution of the war were such that any move our brigade made towards coming to grips with the enemy were to be made as confusing and as frustrating as possible.

Now of course, we would be moving as a brigade, or so we thought, and the ensuing confusion promised to be on a much larger scale. There were to be as many orders and counter-orders as would fool not only the enemy but everyone else associated with the move, including ourselves, and to add to the chaos, most of our movements were to be carried out in the blackout.

The simple but amusing drawing of Mr Chad, whose head, nose and two hands appeared at the top of a wall, seemed to be everywhere, drawn in chalk or paint on any convenient surface or wall, in the streets, the railway stations and even in the public conveniences. He was the enemy agent, watching and listening to all our conversations and we were all told 'Be like Dad, keep Mum' or 'Walls have ears', etc.

Confidentiality in wartime is all very well and absolutely essential, but the sometimes amateurish cloak and dagger efforts to which we were exposed were almost pathetic. Our move from Staindrop was no exception and according to Corporal Thomas of 'C' Company, who kept a diary of events, the move went as follows:

> We left Staindrop with the usual haversack rations of bread and cheese sandwiches and marched to Winson station some few miles away from Staindrop where we boarded a train at about 11.20 p.m. on 6 April. Eventually we left around 1 a.m. in the morning and arrived, after several long halts in various sidings and in the pitch darkness of the blackout on the train *en route*, at Rosyth, on Sunday 7 April.
>
> Here we boarded the destroyer *Afridi* and this was where all the NCOs were issued with maps of Norway, but these were on such a large scale as to be useless, also they were completely out of date and were collected up later on.
>
> We were then ordered off the *Afridi* after a few hours and were re-embarked in the cruiser *Devonshire*.

The following day, 8 April, we were given one hour's notice to get off the *Devonshire* and it was here, in the general mêlée that followed, that some of our equipment was damaged as it was slung ashore willy-nilly in nets and dropped onto the quayside. Some of our supplies were left on board in the heat of the moment, including vital signalling equipment and ammunition as the Navy ships left hurriedly for the North Sea. We then marched through the town of Dunfermline and a further nine miles or so to camp where we went under canvas.

The reason for this sudden activity by the Navy was said at that time to have been due to the sighting of several enemy transports moving within Norwegian territorial waters. One of these ships, the *Rio de Janeiro* of 20,000 tons, was torpedoed in the Skaggerak, off the south coast of Norway (Map 2) after failing to stop when challenged by the Polish submarine *Orzel*. Bodies of German troops and horses were discovered floating in the sea by astonished Norwegian fishermen. Some of the troops were rescued and what a strange tale they had to tell the Norwegian fishermen. The Germans said they were bound for Bergen and Trondheim to defend Norway against an impending invasion by the British and French. The witches' cauldron was on the point of boiling and the Nazis were stirring the brew.

Midnight on 8/9 April was dark and moonless and in the Oslofjord it was so dark that it almost concealed the dim shapes of German transport ships and the naval squadron escorting them along the fjord on their grim mission of invading an unsuspecting country.

The skipper of a plucky little whalecatcher attacked one of the nearest ships with its small 75 mm gun and was almost blown out of the water by a salvo from an enemy cruiser, but at least the Norwegians had been alerted to the fact that they were being invaded.

The capital, Oslo, had no time to resist or even mobilise the army and while German aircraft kept watch overhead, Junkers Ju 52 transport planes and airliners landed at Fornebu airport discharging troops and equipment. German sea transports in the Oslofjord had been attacked by the guns at Horten. They had discharged their troops on the east and west banks of the fjord from whence they proceeded north towards Oslo on motorcycles and in armoured cars and trucks.

Without warning of any kind, or declaration of war and in the dead of night, the Nazis had launched an all-out attack on every strategic point and coastal town throughout the land. This was invasion of a neutral country by stealth and it signalled the end of the 'phoney' war.

Early on the same morning, 9 April, German paratroops had been dropped from Ju 52s in the vicinity of Stavanger's Sola airfield. A few shots had been fired by the Norwegians at the paratroops as they floated earthwards. As the paratroopers moved into the airport the shooting increased, but the paratroopers rallied and advancing from cover to cover, they very quickly overcame Norwegian resistance and Stavanger airport was soon in their hands.

Things were beginning to happen very quickly in this unlucky land, for on this fateful day the British 2nd Destroyer Flotilla consisting of the *Hardy*, the leading ship, commanded by Captain B.A. Warburton-Lee, and the *Havoc* and *Hunter*, was patrolling in the vicinity of the Westfjord, between the Lofoten Islands and the Norwegian coast (Map 2). The Captain put ashore two of his officers at a pilot station and they reported back to him that at least half a dozen enemy warships had entered Ofotfjord, into which Westfjord leads and on which Narvik is situated.

The Admiralty signalled *Hardy* at about 1 a.m. on 10 April to say that if an attack was carried out they approved it, so the Captain radioed back that he would go in at dawn.

Two hours later the warships led by *Hardy* began their passage along the fjord. The weather was not very good, with a bitter east wind, a heavy mist and a snowstorm.

In about an hour and a half, the squadron arrived off Narvik. Leaving four destroyers to patrol outside, *Hardy* entered the harbour. As she drew nearer many ships came into view, including an enemy destroyer. Torpedoes were quickly fired followed by a huge explosion which reverberated round the surrounding hills. The result of this attack put four enemy warships out of action in addition to six armed merchant ships and an ammunition ship which blew up in the harbour. *Hardy* ran aground and her brave captain died at the scene. *Hunter* was sunk, but the other destroyers managed to get away. So ended the first battle of Narvik, but the beginning of the battle for Norway. We were able to read all about this in the papers and although there was a great sense of loss for the brave captain, there was great jubilation in Britain and a shot in the arm for its people that at last a heavy blow had been struck at the German navy and Hitler's war effort in general.

On our arrival by train in Edinburgh on 7 April, the MT platoon and our own Bren-carrier Platoon had been split from the main body of the battalion. We were dropped off at Leith docks to see to the loading of our tanks and transport. Some of HQ Company were put onto lighters and taken out into the River Forth and put into the liner *Orion* which lay at anchor there. The remainder of the battalion carried on to Rosyth.

Waiting alongside the quay at Leith docks was our transport ship, the 7,000 ton *Cedarbank*. One or two other ships were further along the quay. Then we saw the brand new lorries and Bren carriers lined up and waiting for us to drive them onto the loading nets. We drove our carriers onto the nets placed alongside the ship by *Cedarbank*'s derricks, then stood back and watched as the nets folded round each carrier and lorry and lifted them up into the air and over the deck of the ship, where each one hung for a few moments before disappearing down into the depths of the hold.

After our transport had been loaded onto the *Cedarbank*, our platoon sergeant, Po Chambers, ordered us to follow them down into the holds where we spent the remainder of the morning in the gloomy depths chocking up tracks and wheels and tying the tanks and lorries with chains to the deck.

This was as good an indication as any that we were apparently about to move overseas. A good few of my comrades thought otherwise and still thought of it as an exercise and more than likely we would be moving all the transport back onto the quay by tomorrow. 'It's just an exercise, Lofty,' they said to me, 'After all, the war in Finland is over, so we won't be going there.' But at this stage no-one had thought about Norway.

This is where I was parted, like a good many others, from my kit bag, which I never did see after this, and can only assume that it went aboard the *Cedarbank* with the other huge piles of equipment and kit bags belonging to the rest of the battalion.

Later in the day, we were loaded onto lighters and sent across the Forth to the liner *Orion* which was anchored a short way from the Forth Bridge.

On our arrival at the ship we went aboard through a door in her side and were quickly dispersed into accommodation below deck. Most of the MT and Bren-carrier Platoons were kept together and from then on until 18 April we slaved deep in the holds of the ship sorting out and rearranging stores and equipment under the guidance of Quartermaster Lt Sid Morson and RQMS Halford. They could have done very little about where the derricks unloaded the stuff once it was in the hold.

Now it was our task under the eagle eyes of Po Chambers to square it all up so that the various types of stores and equipment were easily accessible according to their priority. It was hot work; moving heavy gear about deep in the warm interior of the ship meant working in our vests only and the sweat poured off us even then.

There were crates of bully beef, boxes and boxes of ammunition, clothing and webbing and to our utter astonishment, cartons and cartons of blanco and brasso which precipitated a gale of invective from one of our platoon corporals, Len Dunkley from Market Harborough.

'It looks as though we shall have to win this bloody war with bullshit instead of bullets,' he said, with one of those inscrutable looks on his long bovine face. He looked up as yet another netful of stores descended, and as if the Gods had heard his plea, a carton fell off the net as it was descending and hit the deck with a slam, splitting open and scattering its contents far and wide. Some of the packs had burst and we picked up as many packets of cigarettes as we could stuff down our battledress blouses and trouser legs. It was as much as some of us could do to climb back up the ladder out of the hold with our trousers and blouses stuffed with cigarettes past the keen eyes of Po Chambers and RQMS Halford. They knew what had happened all right, but they decided to ignore it.

Lance Corporal Bindley of the MT platoon thought it 'Manna from heaven'. He said afterwards, 'I don't know how many fags 'Nuffy' Hall, Archie Pratt and I brought out of that hold, but climbing back up the ladder with the legs of our trousers stuffed with fags was not easy.'

Meanwhile, as all this was going on, the rifle companies of the Leicesters were still under canvas at Dunfermline and apparently enjoying the concerts in the camp, which helped to take their minds off the war.

On 12 April, according to Corporal Arthur Thomas, they were allowed out of camp for the first time and went to the Carnegie baths. On 13 April they embarked in *Orion* with all their equipment and half the battalion of the Sherwood Foresters. The rest of the Foresters, A and D Companies, were then moved from the cruiser *Glasgow*, and put on board the cruiser *Galatea*, whilst B and C and half of their HQ Company boarded *Arethusa*. All the stores for these units had to be handled and stowed away in the holds of *Orion*.

This was the day that the second battle of Narvik took place between the opposing navies when nine destroyers with the battleship *Warspite* leading steamed into the harbour. It was about midday when the shooting started and by the end of the day seven Nazi destroyers had been put out of action and the shore batteries silenced. Three British destroyers had been damaged in the action. An armed guard rescued the survivors of the destroyer *Hardy,* which had run aground during the first battle of Narvik, and handed about one hundred and twenty German prisoners over to the Norwegian authorities.

Early on 14 April, *Orion* weighed anchor and moved off down the River Forth, her diesel engines making the deck tremble gently underfoot. Several wild rumours had it that we were on our way at last and just to prove that we were still subject to orders from above, a rifle inspection was ordered for HQ Company on the main deck. No sooner was this over and we started to make our way below decks, than the ship's klaxon went for boat drill. Couldn't those silly buggers at the top get anything right? Lifebelts, we were more than constantly reminded, once we were underway, were to be worn at all times, even in our quarters. Most of us by this time had a good idea that Norway was going to be our next landfall.

Some of us were anxious and felt edgy and fearful of the unknown, especially me, having come straight from being a farmer's boy into the army. There was a certain kind of relief that we were at last on our way. But it was not to be; in the event we headed nowhere and by late afternoon we discovered that we were sailing back up the Forth to our previous anchorage.

I don't know what effect this exercise had on my comrades, but the adrenalin that had pumped through my veins in the morning with the prospect of coming to grips with the enemy left me feeling deflated and not a little demoralised by the evening. In fact I began to doubt whether I'd ever have the guts to face them.

It never ceased to puzzle us why signalling lamps flashed almost continuously from ship to shore and vice versa all through the hours of darkness and which were visible for miles around. Yet when we had to embark or disembark from ship to ship it had to be done in the blackout and brought about endless confusion, cursing and shouting and even led to some troops boarding the wrong ship. If so much as a cigarette end glowed in the darkness amongst all this chaos it brought down howls and shouts of 'Put that bloody cigarette out!'

On this particular day when we were sailing around the Forth in the *Orion*, British naval forces disembarked at Namsos, about one hundred miles north of Trondheim (Map 2) and they were followed on 17 April by British troops of 146 Brigade which comprised the 1/4th Lincolnshire, 1/4 Yorks and Lancs and 1/4 KOYLI (King's Own Yorkshire Light Infantry) Battalions, also a detachment of the French Chasseurs des Alpins to free a country which was already virtually occupied.

On 16 April we had a fairly easy day aboard the *Orion*, but this state of affairs was not going to last very long and it had been deemed by Whitehall that the *Orion* was too good a ship to put at risk in Norwegian waters where one or two powerful units of the German fleet had been reported. So it was decided early on the morning of 17 April to remove half the battalion of the Foresters B and C Companies and half the battalion of the Leicesters which comprised A and D Companies, the signals platoon and some other specialists from HQ Company. This movement was again carried out in darkness. There was a swell which caused the smaller ships to heave up and down making the transfer of troops, stores and equipment somewhat hazardous.

A and D companies of the Leicesters under Lt Col Guy German boarded the two anti-aircraft cruisers, the *Carlisle* and the *Curacão* whilst the half battalion of the Foresters boarded the *Arethusa*, these were B and C Companies and half their HQ Company under Col T.A. Ford. In *Galatea* were A and D Companies of the Foresters and the other half of their HQ Company and the brigade commander H de R Morgan and his staff.

This transfer of troops and equipment from one ship to another was yet another ill-considered and hurried operation and vital stores were once again left behind. Equipment which was overlooked included brigade headquarters wireless equipment which included a transmitter,

Cruiser HMS *Galatea.*

and also most of the Foresters' mortar ammunition. At the last moment a battery of Bofors guns was put on board but their predictors were left behind, which rendered them useless. By 7 a.m. or so, the task was complete and one or two of us from the Bren-carrier Platoon watched as the ships pulled away on their journey into the unknown. I began to wonder if it was all just another exercise and whether perhaps in an hour or so they would be back and we would have to go through the stupid routine all over again.

At about this time the German paratroopers at Stavanger airport were given orders to block the line of advance of any British troops moving south from Aandalsnes to Oslo and were to be dropped in the Gudbrandsdal valley near to the railway junction of Dombaas (Map 2). They were to prevent Norwegian troops holding out north of Oslo from linking up with the British invasion forces which might be landed on the coast.

The Ju 52s carrying the paratroops took off from Stavanger airport on the afternoon of 17 April and the drop was made just south of Dombaas, some ninety miles in front of the German line advancing north from Oslo. Because of fog, the planes had some difficulty and failed to make their approach to the dropping zone and the paratroopers floated down into deep snow. The transports were spotted by the Norwegians, who opened fire on them. Bullets whipped down the valley from the Norwegian machine-guns and one Ju 52 was blown apart by a direct hit from an anti-aircraft gun. The paratroopers had been scattered by the action and mode of drop, but as many men as possible that could be rounded up were hastily assembled and when a final count was taken, there were sixty-one of them.

Moving down the road which ran through the valley, the depleted force of paratroopers came under heavy machine-gun fire. It appeared that the paratroopers had been dropped into the middle of a locality defended by a Norwegian unit which was both alert and quick on the trigger.

The paratroopers withdrew from the road to establish a defensive position on the slopes of one of the mountains above Dombaas and which dominated the valley. Once they had dug themselves in they returned to the offensive, sending out patrols to seek out and clear the nearest Norwegian positions.

Fifteen Ju 52s had flown the unit into action and of these, eight had gone off course or had been shot down by the Norwegians, yet the paras had carried out their orders and were in a position to intercept both road and rail communications between Dombaas and the south.

In the course of the next few days they inflicted many casualties on the Norwegians and harassed them continually with patrols and raids. Some of the patrols clashed with British troops advancing southwards down the valley from Aandalsnes. But after four or five days of operations, their ammunition was running low and the remaining thirty or so paratroops had no alternative but to surrender.

The situation in Norway at this time was changing rapidly day by day for the worse. The Germans had occupied Oslo, Bergen, Stavanger and Trondheim and the quickly put together Norwegian army, under General Ruge (pronounced Rooga) holding on to positions north of the capital, was faced by a precarious situation. Its morale, as reported by the British liaison officer to the Norwegian army, Colonel E.J. King-Salter, was under very heavy pressure. Quislings and fifth columnists were spreading confusion among the troops and hampering their efforts to stem the advance of the Germans.

The Norwegians, because of the treacherous tactics of their enemy, never really stood a chance. They'd had no time to call up their men and those that had made the effort to assemble found that their depots were already occupied by the enemy, so they were unable to get at their arms and equipment.

On 5 February, a British plan was formulated to rescue the Finns from the Russians. Narvik, Namsos, Trondheim and Bergen were to be occupied (Map 1a) but a second plan which Churchill christened Operation Wilfred (after the smallest member of the cartoon in the *Daily Mirror* Pip, Squeak and Wilfred) was made whereby Narvik was to be the primary object and Stavanger was to be raided.

It was in furtherance of 'Wilfred' that the 1/8 Sherwood Foresters embarked in HMS *Glasgow* at Rosyth on 7 April, just two days before the Germans struck at Norway. That same evening, a third plan was made in London which was to make Narvik the immediate objective to explore the possibility of getting a foothold at Namsos and Aandalsnes. This time, 146 Brigade with 24 Guards Brigade were to go for Narvik, and 148 Brigade for Namsos (Map 1a) but the successes of the Royal Navy at Narvik on 10 April and later on the 13th brought about yet another change of plan and on the evening of the 13th, the War Office authorised the diversion of 146 Brigade from Narvik to Namsos and 148 Brigade from Namsos to Aandalsnes, which now became Plan 4.

The fifth plan of action for employing British and French forces in Norway reached Brigadier H de R Morgan on 17 April whilst he was at sea en route for Norway. It stated briefly, 'Your role to land Aandalsnes, secure Dombaas (Map 2) then operate northwards and take offensive action against the Germans in the Trondheim area.'

Aerial view of Aandalsnes and Romsdal Fjord.

Even after this plan had been radioed to Brigadier Morgan at sea, the War Office had yet another afterthought and another signal was sent to *Galatea* from the Chief of the Imperial General Staff (General Ironside) which read 'When you have secured Dombaas, you are to prevent the Germans from using the railway to reinforce Trondheim.' This brilliant instruction was issued, even though it was a well known fact that every day the Germans were reinforcing Trondheim with troops by air. The signal continued 'You should make contact with Norwegian GHQ, believed to be in the area of Lillehammer, and assist the Norwegian forces operating towards Oslo' (Map 2).

Now Brigadier Morgan had a problem created by these paperwork people. They issued the instructions then completely forgot the plan of action. How could the brigadier operate towards Trondheim and at the same time march south to help the Norwegian army? Somehow, he was expected to do all this with only half a brigade, or one and a half battalions, roughly 1,200 men. The other half of the Leicesters Battalion, which would give him another 400 men, was still in Scotland awaiting instructions to sail. His third battalion, the South Wales Borderers, which would have given him a full brigade, had been taken off him and sent to Narvik with the Guards regiments.

Up to this point, 148 Brigade's first objective had been to secure Dombaas. The next move should have been northwards towards Trondheim to meet up with Mauriceforce under the command of General Carton de Wiart, thereby entrapping the occupying German forces estimated at about 3,000 men. It all looked so easy on paper but the continued plan-making and interference by the brasshats in Whitehall with the commanders in the field only made things more difficult and in the end rubbished the whole expedition and almost destroyed 148 Brigade in casualties and prisoners taken by the enemy. But this wasn't the only mess they made; Dunkirk was to follow shortly afterwards and the mess was on a much larger scale but the politicians weren't having that. They called it the 'miracle of Dunkirk' and then the 'victory', which prompted Dr Goebbels, the German Propaganda Minister, to ask, 'Why do the British always turn their defeats into victories?' And Dunkirk was a defeat, there is no doubt about that.

Brigadier Morgan had no sooner landed at Aandalsnes than a telephone call reached him from the British Military Attaché with General Ruge, Lt Col E.J. King-Salter, who stated that unless some help was made available now, Norwegian resistance would almost certainly collapse. At Dombaas, King-Salter informed the brigadier personally that the War Office had that very day given General Ruge a call on 148 Brigade and that the general's orders were that the British should proceed at once to reinforce the Norwegian army operating at the mouth of the Gudbrandsdal valley. The brigadier, facing up to the inevitable, gave his orders accordingly and then accompanied King-Salter to Norwegian GHQ at Oyer. (Map 3).

After the one and a half battalions of 148 Brigade sailed out of the River Forth on the morning of 17 April, we of the MT and Bren-carrier Platoons were set to work once more in the holds of the *Orion* removing the remaining stores and equipment which we had sorted and stacked for the anticipated voyage overseas only a few days before. The stores were loaded into the nets this time in the hold and the ship's derrick took them up and over the side, where they were dropped into the lighters and taken across the Forth to Leith docks to be stored in the holds of the *Cedarbank*. In all this movement from ship to ship it is hardly surprising that some stores were left behind and others damaged.

This job occupied us until about midday on 19 April when early in the afternoon some of us found ourselves aboard a Chinese cargo boat in the docks, watching some of the crew very seriously playing Mah Jong in the warm sun on the main deck, and wondering if and when we were going to follow the rest of the battalion in this boat to God only knew where!

By the time evening came, we discovered that sailing was not for us and we were marched off into Edinburgh to spend the night in one of the buildings of George Watson's school, the floor of which was already strewn with straw-filled palliasses and pillows.

Coastal vessel *St Magnus*.

19

The following morning we marched to Waverly Station, where we had some hot tea and yes, more cheese sandwiches on the station before boarding a train. When it finally pulled out the morning was well gone and after passing over the Forth bridge, from where we looked down on the toy-sized *Orion* at anchor far below, the train pulled into Dunfermline station. Here the rest of the Leicesters B and C companies boarded it and we continued on our way to Aberdeen but at that particular moment we had no idea where the train was going. Our officers may have known, but they weren't saying. I remember looking out of the carriage windows as we approached Aberdeen just after midday on 20 April and seeing the snow lying about on the hills and mountains beyond in the north-west.

On arrival in the city, we were taken to one of the large restaurants in Union Street where we were given a hot meal. There were so many of us that we had to eat in relays but it was substantial and long overdue.

It was a grey, cold sort of day with lowering black clouds darkening the sky all around as we marched to the docks; a warning of the storm to come.

The fishwives were busy on the quayside at the harbour gutting and cleaning the herrings as we passed by. They laughed and chattered among themselves as they worked. We marched past them and approached two coastal cargo boats waiting for us further along the quayside. Their names stand out in my memory. The nearest one, which we of the MT and Bren-carrier Platoons boarded along with B Coy, was the *St Magnus.* The other one onto which went C Coy with some Sherwood Forester drivers and some sappers was given the unusual name of *St Sunniva.* As we filed on board we were each given one of the now familiar cork lifejackets; most unwieldy things but we found that they made good pillows and would no doubt stand up to any emergency which might befall us in the future. Each coaster must have been at least 200 to 250 feet in length but a few more than a company of men would have crowded it. The *St Magnus* had a single cargo deck and it smelt very strongly as though it had been used for carrying potatoes. This deck was immediately beneath the main deck and was reached by a fairly wide companionway comprising about half a dozen steps and situated about midships. From this deck, it was possible for me to stand up and look out over the main deck to the sea. Being six foot three, I had to be careful not to bang my head when I stood up. Fore and aft beneath the main deck there was more accommodation in the form of fitted bunks, in tiers one above the other. In the stern were located the heads and a washbasin. From what I remember the forequarters were occupied by the crew and the stern bunks were given over to the NCOs of HQ and B Coys. There were no bunks or even hammocks for the other ranks on the cargo deck and I eventually found myself somewhere in the middle of it about a yard or so from the companionway, surrounded by my comrades of the MT and Bren-carrier Platoons and further inboard by the men of C Coy.

We very soon settled down and most began to drop off to sleep and others set up a school of card games. A voice from the galley told us there was bully beef stew available, or tea if preferred, so I spoilt myself and had my dixie filled with strong tea which was so hot and strong I couldn't drink much of it. I threw it into the sea and went back and spread my overcoat on the deck to make a sort of mattress with my equipment and lifejacket providing a pillow. Shortly after we had settled down the coaster's engines began to vibrate and Len Dunkley, whose bed was just alongside mine, began to air his views of our present situation.

'This is it Lofty, have you made your will out?'

'No way, Dunk, for I won't believe it until it actually happens.'

We had left the quayside and stood out to sea with the *Sunniva* and the *Cedarbank*, apparently awaiting our destroyer escorts HMS *Javelin* and HMS *Jackal.*

It must have been about eight o'clock in the evening when we felt the engines vibrate again through the deck boards. As they opened up, the ship moved through the water with a gentle rocking motion on her journey to the open sea. This very soon had most of my comrades asleep and snores could be heard from all sides. Most of us had settled down with our heads to starboard and feet to port. Others lay facing fore and aft but it made very little difference, for as the ship entered the open sea a gale of wind arose and the waves became much rougher and the gentle rocking swiftly changed to a violent pitching and rolling. By this time most of the troops were asleep, but for some reason sleep eluded me and I lay awake listening to the gale that suddenly seemed to have got up, slapping the waves violently against the hull of the ship. Eventually, I fell into an uneasy sleep but was soon awakened by someone stumbling over me to get to the deck rail on the main deck to be sick. The moans and groans of those who had been seasick or felt ill kept me awake for most of the night. It was beginning to get light when I struggled into my boots and made for the companionway to get on deck, but by the time I got there I was already feeling queasy in my stomach and grabbed the deck rail frantically as my last meal came up into my mouth and disappeared in a stream into the depths of the angry ocean. I hung on to the deck rail desperately hoping that I would be better now that I had got rid of last night's meal, but that was just wishful thinking and nothing to do with the reality of the moment. After a few more rolls of the boat my stomach retched again uncontrollably but nothing appeared and I was left gasping with the exhaustion from the effort. I gripped the deck rail frantically and began to sweat. I retched again and this time I quickly realised that I would have to get down the deck to the heads. I hung on to the deck rail and as I made my way down the deck, the sea was boiling like some monstrous cauldron and washing past me on the deck from the bows, the full force of the gale buffeting against me as I struggled onwards to the stern. I eventually arrived at the top of the narrow steps which led down to the stern quarters and the toilet facilities and no sooner had I put my foot on the first step downwards than an assortment of stenches assailed my nostrils and hit me in the face like a blast of hot air from an oven. At the bottom of the steps, the door of the lavatory was swinging open and then slamming violently closed again with the sudden movements of the ship adding other smells to those of sweat and vomit. But I had to go on, driven relentlessly by the unforgiving forces of nature, down to the bottom of the steps. Here, a pathetic scene met me head on. My NCO comrades, who had been allocated to these exclusive but absolutely grim quarters of the boat where the slightest wave movement was multiplied several times over, were hanging over the sides of their bunks groaning pitifully and retching violently onto the floor of the quarters every few minutes before leaning back with looks of utter exhaustion on their faces. With a horrified grunt, I shot through the door of the heads to do what I had to, then I got out and fled back up the stairs to the main deck, where I spent the next quarter of an hour or so hanging over the deck rail. There was not a soul on deck but a lone sailor keeping watch at the bows of the ship who stood propped up against the bulk of an air vent watching the angry seas ahead. I staggered up to him and leaned against the vent with the object of talking to him and perhaps keeping him company for a while, but the noise of the wind and the roar of the ocean combined made it impossible to talk and before I could open my mouth he bent forward and was violently sick. This was too much for me so I backed away and made for the companionway, for I was obliged to go and lie down. This time I slept for an hour or so, after which time I began to feel a bit better, but I was determined to get back up on deck where I could see the horizon and breathe in the fresh air. It was not long before I was quickly joined by several more of my comrades looking pale and green and eager to part with any food in their stomachs.

It was wild on deck and as I leaned out over the deck rail I gazed into the turbulent scene before my eyes. I could just make out the lean grey shape of one of our escorting destroyers as we sailed onward over the water. Looking back over the stern, I watched spellbound as *Sunniva*, the other coaster carrying C Coy of the Leicesters and some Sherwood Forester drivers, seemed to disappear completely beneath the waves for a few seconds to emerge again from one of the huge troughs in the ocean which had swallowed her up. Behind *Sunniva*, I could see the huge hulk of the *Cedarbank* following on.

By midday, 21 April, the *St Magnus* was tossing about like a cork, her timbers shuddering frighteningly and groaning each time her screw left the water as her bows dipped below the storm-tossed surface, to re-emerge again from the ocean like some giant scoop loaded with seawater which was hurled backwards along the main deck towards the stern, where it vanished overboard and back into the sea, splashing water down the open companionways *en route*. Groans could be heard coming from various parts of the ship as the worsening weather took its toll on us land-lubbers.

I looked up at the dark windblown storm clouds scudding past low overhead and it suddenly occurred to me that somewhere out there, a U-boat could be lurking, waiting to send us and the *St Magnus* to the bottom of the sea. I fingered my lifebelt anxiously wondering if it would save me if I was hurled into the sea by the explosion of a torpedo. Staggering along the deck, keeping a tight grip on the deck rail, I made my way back below decks where I was glad to be sheltered from the howling wind. By about 8 p.m. I made myself as comfortable as possible in the hope that I would eventually fall asleep among my comrades.

Keith Lockton, who was a member of the regimental band and served under PSM 'Drummy' Gilbert in the ack-ack platoon later on, remembered the crossing from Aberdeen to Aandalsnes as being terrible: especially for him because the only cooking facility available was a stove to boil water for tea making and the only food he had was bully beef and biscuits, which on the second day made him seasick; it made a lot of us seasick.

Somehow, I at last managed to fall asleep, but it was an uneasy sleep with vivid dreams. In nearly all my dreams I find that the closer I am to waking up the more realistic they are and this time I found myself back at home at that Christmas party where someone burst a balloon close to my ears and the sudden noise of it bursting awakened me instantly. For a moment or so I was puzzled to find that I was not at home, but surrounded by what appeared to be a forest of khaki trousers clad in the usual web anklets. It was only just turned daylight and perhaps about four or five in the morning when I found my voice and shouted up to Len Dunkley, who was standing just by me.

'What's going on, Len?' I asked, grabbing my lifejacket and getting quickly to my feet, already beginning to fear the worst. 'Why is everyone standing up?' I persisted.

'Our transport ship, *Cedarbank* has just been torpedoed,' he said grimly, 'Didn't you hear the bang?' God, it was loud enough to waken the dead.'

'Well – I heard something,' I gasped, pulling my equipment on, 'but I thought I'd dreamt it.'

'This is no dream, mate, it's a wonder you weren't trampled underfoot in the panic with everyone trying to get on deck at once – we all thought this bloody boat had been hit – but we were sent back below and told to stay there.'

'Where is it?' I asked nervously, craning my neck to see over the companionway.

'Over there,' he said, 'if you look now you might be just in time to see it disappear.' My eyes followed the direction of his pointing finger and no sooner had I focused on the huge bows rearing up out of the water than she vanished into the deep amidst a swirl of angry foam.

Then came another huge explosion, shaking every timber in the *St Magnus* and causing a hum of frightened voices amongst my comrades. I struggled quickly into my kit and tied my lifebelt around my waist.

'That was a depth charge from one of the destroyers,' someone muttered at length, but the remark did little to ease the nervous tension.

When we were able to get on deck again we could quite plainly see one of the destroyers circling around a certain spot on the surface and every now and then firing off depth charges which looked like fifty-gallon oil drums on the end of a broom handle. They came off each side of the destroyer's deck at about forty-five degrees and hurtled up into the air, before falling back into the sea, where they sank beneath the surface for a few minutes before erupting in a huge waterspout followed by a dull thud somewhere below.

The other destroyer was circling the remainder of our little convoy at speed now and much closer than they had been before. All this was interesting for us to watch but it did nothing for our morale, it only made me wonder when and where the next torpedo would strike.

Even after sixty years, I can still hear the voice of 'Crusty' Curtis, one of the MT platoon drivers standing close by me and moaning about all our kit being on that boat: lorries, Bren carriers, rations, ammo and all.

'Yes, and all that bloody brasso and blanco,' said Len Dunkley. 'We're going to have to try and beat Jerry without all that bullshit now.' There were a few chuckles from our comrades at this outburst from Len.

'I wonder what happened to the crew?' Nuffy Hall asked, 'She only took about ten minutes to sink, they wouldn't have had much time to get off.' Nuffy was a caring person, a down to earth chap who was nobody's fool.

We heard afterwards that there had been about sixty crew, out of which some twenty-eight had been picked up by the destroyers, four of whom had later died of burns.

Suddenly, a great silence came down upon us like a blanket as a fit of depression overcame the troops after the recent events, which brought home to most of us the meaning of war and that whatever else had been on the *Cedarbank*, we now had only our rifles, a few anti-tank rifles and Bren guns to face the enemy with, also the clothes we stood up in; one battledress and one great coat. The gloom was so deep that Jackie Newton, from Quorn, and a member of the band, got his saxophone out and started playing 'Roll out the barrel' and a few other cheerful tunes to try and raise our spirits. We needed it as we watched the destroyers which were still steaming round, dropping the odd depth charge in the hope of hitting the U-boat. Amidst all this going on, a shout came from one of the sailors on watch.

'Mine ahead, mine ahead, off port bow,' he yelled, pointing seawards. We all looked fearfully in the direction of his pointing finger and wondered if we were on the point of being blown up by this new menace. Sure enough, we saw the round black top of the mine bobbing slowly up and down in the sea, complete with some of its sinister spikes sticking out of its body, almost willing the *St Magnus* to draw nearer. We watched petrified with fear as the mine passed down the length of our boat but a few yards away and as it passed the stern another sailor came on deck with a 303 rifle and commenced firing at it from the deck rail. The general excitement and the noise of the rifle fire brought a few more Leicesters on deck with pale, sickly looking faces and no sooner had some of them caught a glimpse of the sea than they had to rush to the deck rail to hang over it heaving and retching.

By this time, the mine was some hundred yards away before a lucky shot from the sailor hit one of the spikes on the mine in the right place, for there was a sudden brilliant flash and an almighty crack of an explosion which made the old *St Magnus* tremble in every timber and shot a waterspout some thirty feet into the air. A cheer went up from those of us on deck who were watching the proceedings with a certain amount of temerity and were very thankful to have been spared a fate similar to that which befell the *Cedarbank* but there was no guarantee that we were out of immediate danger for as Len Dunkley said:

'That was one of our own mines would you believe, broken free from a minefield laid by our mine laying ships just off the Norwegian coast, to sink enemy ships using the "leads", I remember reading about it in the papers back home.'

Shortly after this incident it began to snow huge snowflakes and before we knew what was happening we were enveloped in a blizzard, the likes of which I had never seen before and which completely obliterated everything beyond a few yards. The storm raged for about half an hour or so and the giant snowflakes ceased falling just as quickly as they'd started. The sun very shortly broke through the clouds and blue skies appeared, bringing a few more Leicesters up on deck. I shivered in the sub-arctic morning and thought that we were naked soldiers in more ways than one. All I had to defend myself with was my Lee-Enfield rifle and one hundred rounds of ammunition in two cloth fifty-round bandoliers. When these had gone, I had nothing and my comrades were similarly placed.

It must have been in the region of 6 a.m. when we first noticed the huge black, evil-looking mountains which rose straight up out of the sea and disappeared skywards into an all concealing mist.

'Well at least we know where we are, lads, for with mountains like those it's got to be Norway,' Po Chambers said grimly, 'and God knows what we are going to do without our transport.'

A school of porpoises attracted a lot of attention as they swam past the boat, splashing playfully about in the water. By this time the wind had died down and the sea had lost most of its ferocity and most of us crammed the deck rails admiring the wild-looking scenery which passed by us like some slowly unfolding film, and by this time most of us knew it was Norway.

By about seven o'clock we had reached the mouth of the Romsdal Fjord and this was where one of our escorting destroyers left us to patrol the mouth of the fjord while the other one escorted us along the fjord to Aandalsnes. As we sailed up the fjord the surface was like a millpond, smooth and glassy, and there were many shouts of surprise and admiration as the unusual scenery came into view.

'Cor! Look at that farm, mate,' Lance-Corporal Bindley gasped in disbelief, 'It's almost carved out of the mountainside.' We looked to where he was pointing at a natural shelf at the foot of the mountain which was roughly half a mile long by about five hundred yards in width and sloped gently down to the water's edge. It had its own little beach with a rowing boat lying on the sand nearby. The land was covered with a yellowish grass on which were dotted the white woolly bodies of some sheep with a cow or two grazing amongst them. On one side of the shelf was a collection of timber-built buildings which gave it the status of a small farm.

As we progressed up the fjord, we noticed several of such small holdings and wondered how the occupants obtained access to them from the land side, which to us on the boat looked almost impossible.

The sun shone with a little warmth in it now and as the day grew older we heard the drone of an aircraft high up in the blue sky above us.

'Righto lads!' came the voice of Sergeant Chambers, 'Get back down below and get your kit on for we'll be landing in just about fifteen minutes. Make sure your rifles are loaded with ten rounds in the magazine for we don't know what sort of reception we're going to get.' But Po needn't have worried, for as it happened there were very few Norwegians in the vicinity of the rickety old wooden jetty.

Nevertheless, this announcement sent a tingle of apprehension up and down my spine as I scrambled back down the companionway steps to get my kit. It was about 8 a.m. on the morning of 22 April 1940 when the *St Magnus* made fast against the quayside that served the little town of Aandalsnes, to be closely followed by the *Sunniva*. Our escort turned about and after firing several shots at the intruder in the sky, headed back up the fjord. So this is how we, the second half of the Leicestershire Regiment, arrived in Norway.

There were no crowds to welcome us, but we all had an uneasy feeling that the spy in the sky was already on his radio to arrange a warm welcome for us but we had no way of knowing. The destroyer which had just left us was taking no chances and opened up on it again with its guns. Eventually, it flew off, leaving us to admire the awesome scenery displayed before our eyes. The wild snow-clad hills, their lower slopes hidden in forests of birch and conifers with occasional clearings where a timber building might be seen, all served to remind us that we were now in an alien land and a good five hundred miles from home.

THREE

148 BRIGADE DEPLOYS

As stated earlier, 148 Brigade was at this point code-named Operation Sickleforce after the route of the railway from Aandalsnes via Dombaas to Trondheim where it would link up with Mauriceforce (146 Brigade) moving south from Namsos.

In his account of the part his battalion, the 1/8 Sherwood Foresters, played in the early days of the campaign Captain E.C.G. Beckwith, OC A Company, the Sherwood Foresters, attempts to simplify the actions and refers to B and C companies under CO Col Ford and A and D companies of the 1/5th Leicesters under CO Col German as East Force and to the 2nd i/c Sherwood Foresters Major Roberts's half of the battalion, comprising A and D companies, as West Force.

At about 8 p.m. on 18 April, *Arethusa* and *Carlisle* berthed at Molde, on the north side of the Romsdal Fjord (Map 2). The landing, contrary to expectations, was unopposed and within an hour all men were disembarked and the two cruisers slipped away. The troops dispersed into the nearby woods and the ruins of the town, which had been heavily bombed during the day.

The cruisers having departed, five coastal vessels came alongside the jetty, one of which had the unusual name of *Black Swan*, and we proceeded for the next three hours to load troops and stores into them for crossing to Aandalsnes, some twenty miles further up the fjord on the south side. Meanwhile *Galatea* and *Curacão* made for Aandalsnes. Captain Beckwith said:

> It is doubtful if any who were present then could easily forget the thrill of that spring evening, while the ships slipped silently along as though threading their way through a deep canyon with the darkening glow of a starlit night overhead. The surface of the fjord was smooth and glassy but we felt the icy chill on the deck and from the snow clad slopes of the mountains closing in nearer and nearer as the fjord narrowed while the Norwegian pilot led a breathless convoy in line ahead towards our destination.
>
> Shortly before 10 p.m. *Galatea* slid quietly to rest alongside the little wooden tourist jetty at Aandalsnes. There had been no signs of opposition from the Norwegians and in the starlight we could see crowds swarming

Captain E.C.G. Beckwith,
OC A Coy Foresters.

down to the waterfront to greet us. We shivered a little but were thankful
of the fact that 'Sickleforce' had arrived at last, even though we might have
been regarded by some as invaders.

By 11 p.m. disembarkation was completed. Some Royal Marines who
had landed from HMS *Hood* on the previous evening, took A Company
(CO Major Roberts) and half of HQ Company to billets in the vicinity
of the landing stage. A party of A Company was kept on the quay to sort
and load ammunition and stores onto a train. The company was billeted
in a school and by 1 a.m. got down to some welcome sleep.

At Aandalsnes news awaited the brigadier. The Norwegians were
holding the Germans astride Lake Mjosa some hundred miles to the
south, but he also learned that German paratroops had been dropped at
about 6.30 p.m. on 17 April in the high mountains a short distance south
of Dombaas railway station. They had lost a lot of men in the landings,
but about sixty Germans were holding out in a farmhouse covering the
railway line.

Brigadier Morgan acted quickly. By midnight, D Coy (Major Kirkland) were entrained and about an hour later, with the brigade staff and Major Roberts, were away for Dombaas, which they reached about 4 p.m. 19 April. A Company was organised for AA defence and put under cover, the brigadier meanwhile went off to reconnoitre down the line in a locomotive and one coach.

By this time East Force had sailed from Molde in five coastal vessels and berthed at Aandalsnes by 2.30 a.m. By the time they had unloaded stores onto an already packed quayside, loaded what they needed and had all been trucked out to an improvised camp, some five miles from the town, it was nearly noon on 19 April. The troops were fed and looked forward to some sleep, but by 3 p.m., having reloaded the trucks, B and C Companies and half the battalion of the Leicesters were on the march back to the station to entrain.

At 8 a.m. that Friday morning, A Coy (Captain Beckwith) had reported as ordered at the station. Apart from a visit by a German recce plane at breakfast (compo rations), there had been no alarms. But now a train came in from Dombaas, empty except for Brigadier Morgan and Col Dudley Clarke (Liaison Officer to the War Office).

A company was ordered aboard the train and warned to expect trouble from paratroops and hostile aircraft and by 11.30 a.m. was on its way south. At the last moment the brigadier joined the train as he had just received some very disquieting news from the Norwegian front.

At about 2.30 p.m. A Coy arrived at Dombaas station but the men were not allowed to detrain and half an hour later the train moved off again southwards accompanied by OC West Force Major Roberts and his acting adjutant (Lieutenant Bradley). D company was ordered to follow as soon as another train could be obtained. The paratroops at Dombaas had by this time surrendered and the line was clear.

Up to this point, 148 Brigade's objective had been to secure Dombaas. The next move should have been northwards towards Trondheim to meet up with 'Mauriceforce' under the command of General Carton de Wiart thereby entrapping the occupying German forces estimated at around 3,000 men. But that morning a telephone call had reached the brigadier at Aandalsnes from King-Salter, the British Military Attaché with General Ruge. He stated that unless some help was made available now, Norwegian resistance would almost certainly collapse. At Dombaas King-Salter informed the brigadier personally that the War Office had that day given General Ruge a call on 148 Brigade and that the general's orders were that the British should proceed at once to reinforce the Norwegian army at the mouth of the Gudbrandsdal valley. The brigadier, facing up to the inevitable, gave his orders accordingly and then accompanied King-Salter to Norwegian GHQ at Oyer (Map 3).

On arrival at Oyer, they found that not a single car, motorcycle or even

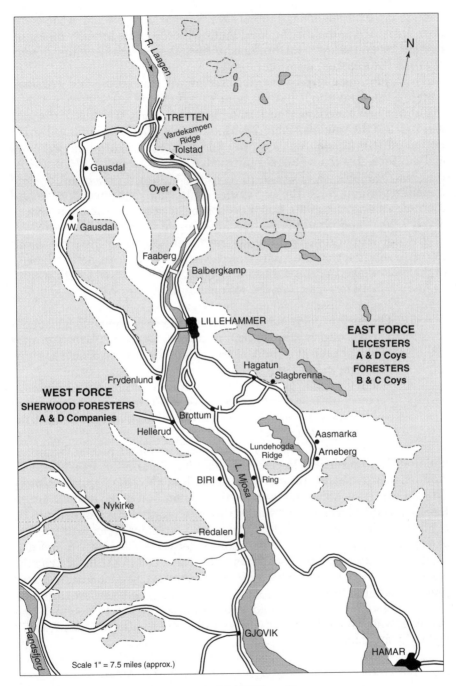

Map 3   Main battle area and location of the two battalions.

a sentry gave the slightest hint that they were in the presence of the GHQ of an army. It was their first experience of the elaborate security measures needed to defeat the Quislings, who had at first betrayed their every move to the German air force.

By 11 p.m. that Friday evening, East Force Leicesters and Foresters were on the train about half an hour's travel south of Dombaas, where the troops had been issued with bully beef and blankets. Most of the men were in freight wagons, there being only two coaches. D Coy, having entrained at Dombaas at 5 p.m. and sat for an hour in a siding, were still an hour's journey from Faaberg (Map 3). A Coy, with half HQ Company, reached Faaberg at about 7 p.m., after having been bombed and machine-gunned from the air *en route* and had detrained and shifted themselves and their kits and stores into lorries. They left Faaberg at about 7 p.m., and swung down the west side of Lake Mjosa, a vast sheet of grey ice in the moonlight, and some two hours later arrived at Biri (Map 3), where the column halted and Major Roberts reported to the HQ of the Norwegian Dahl Force for orders. By this time it was freezing hard.

At Biri, Roberts was given the following information:

1. The enemy was at present held south of Gjovik (Map 3).
2. The Norwegian force on the west side of Lake Mjosa (Dahl) consisted of one brigade of infantry (3 battalions), one battery of field artillery, engineers and a supply column.
3. Whilst the Norwegian left flank was thought secure, since it rested on the shore of the frozen Lake Mjosa, there was danger to the right from a possible outflanking movement by the German forces driving up the Randsfjord to the west. (Map 3).

Colonel Dahl, commanding the Norwegian troops on this front, ordered Roberts to move his two and a half companies to Nykirke, approximately fifteen miles by road further west, with the intention of covering the right flank of Dahl force. Roberts asked for one company of ski troops to protect the flanks of our own forces. This was considered necessary owing to the depth of snow off road which was some three feet deep. A and HQ Coys (Lieutenant Laing) were ordered to offload all unessential baggage for the next twenty-four hours. The kit was dumped in a barn and a guard placed in charge of it.

The remainder got into trucks and set out for Nykirke, except Major Roberts, who waited for D Coy. The time was just after midnight and it began to snow heavily.

Saturday, 20 April

We left East Force travelling southwards out of Dombaas. At 2.50 a.m. the first train pulled into Lillehammer. Col Ford was met by the brigadier, Col Dudley Clarke and General Ruge. The half Battalion of the Leicesters had been ordered south as far as Tretten. The Foresters got themselves and their kit off the train and by 5 p.m. were dispersed into billets about three miles south of the town. Major B. Dowson and Lt P. Ellis with sixty men got the stores into storage. At the midnight conference at brigade and battalion HQ at the Victoria Hotel in Oyer, General Ruge in his role of C-in-C made his intentions very clear to Brigadier Morgan. Trondheim could wait; the front south of Lillehammer was of paramount importance. If he could hold the Germans there, reinforcements from the UK could build up and eventually drive the Germans back to Oslo. Operations must conform to his strategy. The brigadier had no option but to concur in the immediate plan, but the lines of communication were about 140 miles long and there were no reserves whatever – except for the second half of the Leicesters who were still at sea. Later that day, General Ruge stated that British detachments must comply with the wishes of the C-in-C or else he would resign. He made a comment about the Norwegian forces which does not seem out of place here:

> Remember what kind of army this was. From Oslo for instance, came hundreds of men who could not mobilise because the Germans held the city. They gathered around some leader and became a company; then they met other groups of the same kind and became battalions under the command of some officer. Casually assembled infantrymen, artillery men, sailors and aviators, with cars and chauffeurs collected from God knows where, became fighting units. A commissary department was improvised, the women on the farms doing the cooking. At this time 148 Brigade had no transport of its own.

The information given to the CO at Lillehammer was briefly, that the Norwegians were holding the Germans south of Ring (Lundehogda Ridge, Map 4). The Norwegian Second Division, under General Hvinden Haug, consisted of one part battalion of infantry, a battalion of ski troops and a battery of artillery, about five hundred men in all. There was also a Norwegian Dragoon Regiment of about one thousand men which was engaged in the area of Arneberg (Map 4) south of Aasmarka, under the command of a Colonel Jensen. At 10 a.m. Colonel Ford reported to General Hvinden Haug at his HQ north of Ring (Map 3). Here he was told that while there was pressure on the Norwegian front, there was no breakthrough. The CO was asked if he could spare any weapons. He offered one 3 in mortar section and two anti-tank rifle

33

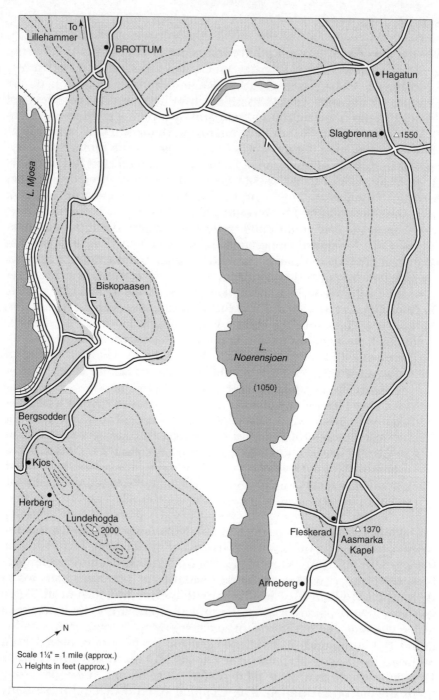

Map 4   Kjos and Bergsodder, also Arneberg and Aasmarka.

sections, which were accepted. Lt H. Dolphin and a Leicesters officer were nominated as liaison officers with the Norwegians. Lt Ellis of C Coy became battalion transport officer.

On his way back to Lillehammer Col Ford called in on his two Company Commanders B Coy Capt. P. Branston and C Coy Capt. M. Redmayne and gave them their orders. East Force was to move south to Brottum (Map 3) in support of the Norwegians at Ring. At about 2 p.m. the CO took his Coy Commanders to reconnoitre the new position and then returned with them to battalion HQ at the Victoria Hotel for a conference. It was by then 5 p.m. The troops had been given about twelve hours' rest, undisturbed except for periodic machine-gun fire from German aircraft searching the woods. All ranks were under orders not to give away their position by returning fire.

Meantime, Col German and his half battalion of Leicesters had arrived on the scene. They had detrained at Tretten at about 10.30 a.m. and had been brought forward by lorry and bus through Lillehammer to Brottum after having been misdirected by a suspected Quisling, and had been machine-gunned from the air from a low height, but fortunately suffered no casualties. General Hvinden Haug seemed surprised to see them; they had, he said, come too far, but as it happened, he had a job for them.

Having withdrawn the troops to billets near Lillehammer that evening, Col German with Brigadier Morgan and Col Dudley Clarke took the hill road inland to meet Col Jensen and his Dragoons at Aasmarka.

The Norwegians were undoubtedly wearied by ten days of continual movement and the occupation of successive defensive positions, but the Germans seemed to have been content to push them back from one to another with no attempt to do more than follow up in a leisurely fashion. As a result, the Dragoons had suffered very few casualties and lack of rest was their only real complaint.

At 9 p.m. that Saturday evening the CO got into his car again and was driven over the snow-bound country road back to 2nd Div HQ north of Ring. Here he was told that the Norwegians had suffered considerable casualties. The Norwegian divisional commander gave orders for the British to relieve the forward troops (Foresters at Lundehogda, the Leicesters at Aasmarka. Map 3) at 2 p.m. on the following day, the 21st. Col Ford agreed with the Norwegians the positions for the 3 in mortar and the Boyes 0.5 in anti-tank rifles. The 3 in mortar, protected by one anti-tank (A/T) section to the NW of Kjos (Map 4) under the crest of Lundehogda, the second A/T rifle by the Lakeside south of Bergsodder – and at midnight sent the troops south to occupy them (Map 4). At 10 p.m. B Coy moved south to Brottum, C Coy remaining put outside Lillehammer. All seemed quiet enough.

Meanwhile much activity had occupied A and D Coys on the other side of the lake. A Coy and the HQ Coy element, in spite of a heavy snowstorm, duly reached Nykirke at about 1 a.m. Here, they were informed that the Germans were 'somewhere down the road' and only a ski patrol out in front of them. OC Coy made his dispositions accordingly. Having no motor transport of their own both the Foresters and the Leicesters were entirely dependent throughout the brief campaign on Norwegian civilian drivers. They were brave men but unfortunately we were quite unable to converse with them and we had no maps. Nor had they.

Owing to the utter chaos of transferring from ship to ship in Rosyth, three long days before, West Force signals had the field telephone instruments and East Force had the cable. The all important generator had been left behind in the mêlée, consequently there could be no communication between the two forces. It was not a very satisfactory state of affairs.

At 2 a.m. D Coy picked up Major Roberts at Biri and in due course, joined A Coy at Nykirke, where at first light both companies and the 3 in mortar were put into position to cover the road winding down into the valley. A ridge rose sharply some two to three hundred feet to the right of the position and the snow slopes ran steeply down to a frozen stream to the left. There was a thick pine forest as far as the eye could see (Sketch A). West Force was now deployed with roadblocks in position on the morning of 20 April.

At 11 a.m. a Norwegian Officer informed Major Roberts that Gjovik had fallen. Two hours later the news was confirmed by Col Dahl's HQ and Roberts was ordered to withdraw his force to Biri to avoid being cut off by a rapid German advance up the main Gjovik–Biri road. West Force would be relieved by Norwegian ski troops and would use their transport to get back in. The ski company promised as flank guard to West Force had never shown up, but now at 1.30 p.m. they came. However, their transport was insufficient to lift the two and a half companies and a shuttle service had to be arranged. In view of the German successes at Gjovik, there was some urgency. Major Roberts hurried off to Biri for further orders and to arrange for more transport. D Coy, having had a meal, embussed and at 2.30 p.m. set out for the lake. The remainder, relieved by the Norwegians, got some food and sleep in the church.

D Coy arrived safely at the main road at Redalen (Map 3) debussed and sent the trucks back for A and half HQ Coy. It arrived piecemeal and maddeningly slowly. In view of the threatening situation on the main road, OC A Coy decided to take his company on, leaving HQ to follow as transport arrived. They left Nykirke at 4.30 p.m. The roads were bad and the pace slow. There was no way of knowing whether or not D Coy had been able to make Redalen in time or even if they were still there. For the second half of the journey A Coy travelled with their bayonets fixed. All went well. At Redalen, Major Kirkland reported no sign of

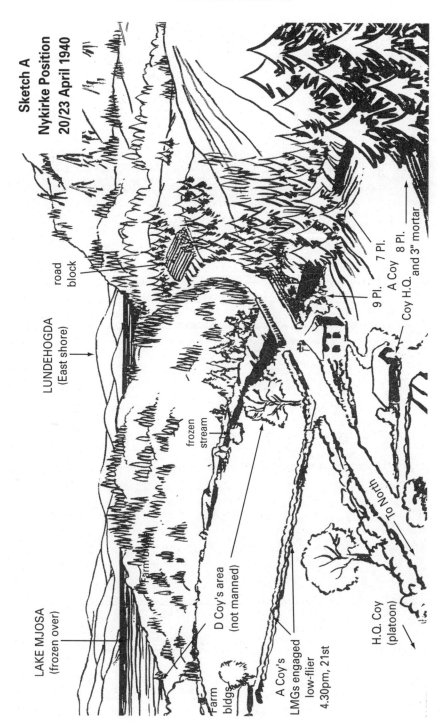

Sketch A
Nykirke Position
20/23 April 1940

LAKE MJOSA
(frozen over)

LUNDEHOGDA
(East shore)

road
block

frozen
stream

Farm
bldgs

D Coy's area
(not manned)

A Coy's
LMGs engaged
low-flier
4.30pm, 21st

9 Pl.

7 Pl.
A Coy 8 Pl.
Coy H.Q.
and 3" mortar

To North

H.Q. Coy
(platoon)

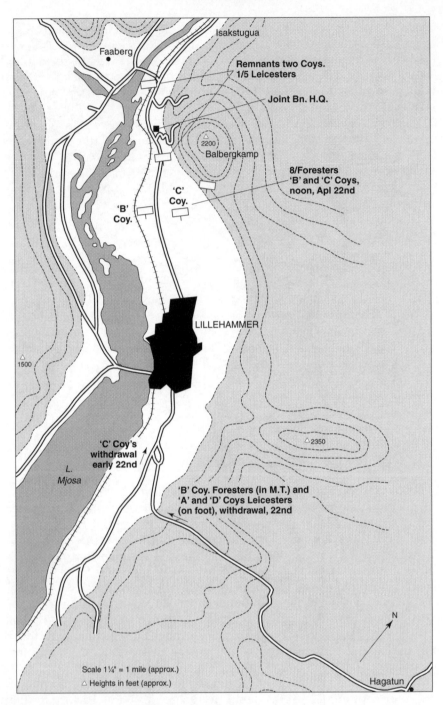

Map 5   Lillehammer and Balbergkamp area.

Germans and directed A on towards Biri. They were finally met by the West Force interpreter, Private Jepson of the Norwegian army. He took them on to Hellerud, ten kilometres north of Biri, where they found Major Roberts. Here A debussed and sent the transport back for D and HQ Coys. It was almost 7 p.m. Three hours later at 10 p.m. the remainder of West Force joined them.

The reader should understand what type of country we were operating in: densely forested heights, the frozen Lake Mjosa and the ever present snow which lay off the road to a depth of three feet and more in places. In addition a steady stream of Norwegian soldiery passing northwards; from their faces and behaviour one would have thought they were following up a retreating enemy. Unfortunately, they were not.

That afternoon at Biri, at the headquarters of Dahl Force, Major Roberts was put in the picture:

1. The enemy had taken Gjovik and crossed to the north bank of the river there.
2. It was the intention of Dahl Force to withdraw northwards.
3. The British troops would become rearguard to Dahl Force and would take up their first position at Hellerud. (Map 3) This position was to be held until the last elements of Dahl Force had passed through and for a period afterwards which would be advised later.

Roberts then requested:

(a) Adequate transport.
(b) A company of ski troops to protect his right (hill) flank.
(c) A detachment of engineers to demolish bridges etc.

He then went on to Hellerud and made a thorough reconnaissance of the position that his troops would have to occupy. At 8 p.m. he returned to Biri, where Col Dahl informed him that he might require one company to hold the River Stokeroen, one kilometre in front of Redalen, the next day 21 April. This would then become the first rearguard position.

Roberts then returned to Hellerud, found that his whole force was once again concentrated, and warned OC D Coy that he might have to move to Redalen at short notice in the event of an alarm coming from the Norwegian front. Part of the unessential baggage of the two and a half companies was sent in a convoy of trucks under Lt Sketchley, now transport officer and acting QM, back to Faaberg railway station. It was now about midnight. West Force was due for some sleep.

As an instance of the 'fog of war' and the general lack of information and inter-communication, it might be recorded that at 10.45 p.m. that night the two company commanders at Hellerud, who had not seen their

CO for several hours and who knew only that he had gone to Biri and could easily have met with some mishap, decided to risk security and put a call through on the public line to the Victoria Hotel in Lillehammer which they had 'heard' was Battalion HQ. Fortunately, the reply came in English and Capt. Beckwith spoke to Major Dowson who said it was lucky he'd rung for they had been wondering what was happening to them.

Sunday, 21 April

At 2 a.m. in the hotel Col Ford, CO of the Foresters, was roused to be told that the Germans had broken through the Norwegian position south of Lundehogda. The situation was very grave. He spoke to Col Clarke, who advised against waking the brigadier. Things were definitely warming up. That morning, the Germans who had been held in both positions the previous day, began a more determined attack for which they had both the motive and the means, for the approach of British troops on the scene destroyed any idea that the operations against the Norwegians would peter out without any serious bloodshed. Army Group Pellengahr was now pushing up the east bank of Lake Mjosa with

Germans advance on Lillehammer.

two infantry battalions, a motorised machine-gun battalion, a battery of artillery and smaller units – a total of some 4,000 men. The Germans also had unchallenged mastery of the air.

Reveille that morning for C Foresters East Force Company was at 3 a.m. and an hour later they moved to a farm south of Brottum and got down to preparing their positions. At the same time B Coy was ordered back half a mile to a position behind and to the right of C, their overnight position clearly being unsuitable, astride a road with no cover to speak of, frozen and with deep snow. Digging was impossible, and they built 'sangars' of rock.

During the morning the Leicesters moved up to the Aasmarka area; being attacked from the air on the road, but without damage. The Foresters HQ personnel under Lt Fitzherbert withdrew to C Coy's old billet near Lillehammer and Battalion HQ moved forward to a school some three miles south of the town.

At 2 p.m. the CO Col Ford was at Norwegian 2nd Div. HQ. He learnt that the Norwegians were preparing to withdraw from the Lundehogda –Aasmarka positions and details were agreed with the Norwegian chief-of-staff. Units would move out in the order: (1) Norwegians; when clear of the roads (2) Leicesters, (3) B Coy Foresters, (4) C Coy Foresters. Col Ford was ordered to cover the Leicesters' withdrawal from Aasmarka.

At 4 p.m., the two company commanders were ordered to meet the CO at a crossroads behind the Leicesters. (Slagbrenna, Map 4). At the rendezvous they found also General Hvinden Haug, who told them that the dragoons would withdraw by the top road – Aasmarka–Hagatun–Lillehammer. The CO decided to leave C Coy at Brottum and to move B Coy up to Slagbrenna.

The Germans were already firing onto the position with artillery and mortars and now they began to outflank the position on both sides through the forest. By day in April the Norwegian snow is like walking through a bog, but by night it freezes solid. In the circumstances, the dragoons held on around Arneberg (Map 3) while the Leicesters established a position in depth just behind Aasmarka. By about 8 p.m. the Norwegians had passed through the Leicesters and had withdrawn northwards, as planned. Fortunately, the Germans did not follow up.

By 5 p.m. that evening, General Hvinden Haug had decided to pull out completely to the north of Lillehammer where a shorter front might prove more easily defensible. But the withdrawal of the Norwegian battalion from Lundehogda via Brottum, beginning in the early evening, opened the way for a German advance along the main Lakeside road and endangered the communications of not only the British companies on the Aasmarka–Hagatun road but also of West Force, of which D Coy was still at Redalen and the remainder at Hellerud.

*   *   *

41

The German attack on Aasmarka had coincided with the bombardment of Lundehogda. Of the Foresters' mortar section there, under Sergeant Gutteridge, it was learnt that German guns were brought to bear on the position and it quickly ceased fire. The section rejoined their unit at 9 p.m. By 10 p.m. B Coy were in their new position, occupying some houses. Meanwhile C at Brottum watched the Norwegian withdrawal and endeavoured to check who was who, but without much success. A Norwegian Red Cross orderly told Capt. Redmayne that the Germans were advancing up the main road. Redmayne got onto a pushbike to inform the CO. At 8 p.m. half the signal platoon had joined C Coy as riflemen.

On the upper road, the two companies of Leicesters were preparing to get out as ordered. It was known that Capt. S.P. Symington and forty-five men were at Aasmarka at 11 p.m. But a time limit fixed for 1 a.m. had been laid down, by which time the troops retiring from Aasmarka must have passed through Lillehammer to avoid being trapped. Unfortunately the only transport available was that taking the Norwegian dragoons to their next halt some twelve miles north of Lillehammer. This transport failed to return for the British troops and Col German and the Leicesters set out to march it.

At 11.30 p.m. that Sunday night Capt. Branston, OC B Coy, who was at Hagatun, was informed that his company was in the wrong position. He accordingly set out south-eastwards with his platoon commanders and Brens No. 1 and 2 along the road. It had been a trying day. While Brottum is a hamlet, Hagatun and Slagbrenna are only farmsteads.

There was now nothing between them and the enemy and their transport had failed to turn up. Branston immediately sent 2nd Lt W. Dixon back in a truck to Battalion HQ to inform Col Ford of the Leicesters' plight. Meanwhile they marched on towards Lillehammer. About 3 a.m. when clear of the crossroads B Coy embussed in their own transport and left for Lillehammer. The run was uneventful and they reached the deserted town where they were met by the Adjutant, Capt. Renwick, picked up some gear and arrived at their rendezvous, the agricultural college two to three miles north of the town at 4.30 a.m. This was the Balbergkamp position (Map 5).

A few hours earlier, around midnight, Col. Ford had told his IO, 2nd Lt Crane, that the battalion was to withdraw to this new position. The 2IC, Major Dowson, was ordered to reconnoitre it and was told that he would meet there a Norwegian officer by the name of Major Brun, but he failed to find him. At 3 a.m. the HQ Coy details under Lt Fitzherbert withdrew through Lillehammer to the agricultural college.

Meanwhile, on the lower road about Brottum, C Coy watched the last of the Norwegians passing through from Lundehogda. Finally, about dawn, nothing more came and for a long time they sat and waited. They were enlivened by the sound of explosions behind them as the long bridge at Lillehammer was blown by Norwegian sappers. At about 3.30 a.m. orders came for C Coy to withdraw through Lillehammer. All went according to plan until they saw down the road to the south about twenty motorcyclists at about eight hundred yards distance. Redmayne said he was in doubt whether to debus the platoon again, but at that moment the motorcycles wheeled off the road and we beat it. The order had been to withdraw without contact if that was possible. C Coy withdrew intact.

But to return to the unfortunate Leicesters on the upper road five miles to the north east of Brottum. After their first day in action, these Territorials had to set out at midnight on a fourteen mile march from Aasmarka over hilly snowbound lanes to Lillehammer; an ordeal whose effects on morale would be heightened by suspicions of Norwegian honesty. A serious setback followed: in the approaches to the town, when it was already daylight, enough transport met the column to carry the majority of the troops through in the nick of time. But the Germans cut off a considerable party, including six officers, and also overran the stores which had been accumulated at the railway station. At the Balbergkamp, two miles north of the town, the Leicestershires, their numbers further reduced by some of the transport overrunning their destination, rejoined the two and a half companies of Foresters. The total of East Force was now about six hundred and fifty officers and men. The transport that had met the Leicesters in the nick of time had been sent by Col Ford with Lt Dixon, who volunteered to go back with the lorries and see whether the Leicesters could be found. This he did successfully and brought them back to the rendezvous.

It is unlikely that anyone in East Force, at least outside Battalion HQ had much thought to spare for the other half battalion west of the lake. A brief study of Map 3 will show just how vulnerable a position they were in. At 4.30 a.m. on that Monday morning, D Coy was still a mile south of Redalen, and the last remnants of Dahl Force was still passing over the Stokeroen bridge. The stream was frozen solid and covered with snow. Though not marked on the map, it runs south of and parallel to the Nykirke/Redalen road. Redalen is by road some 25 miles south of the Balbergkamp and the whole of the east shore up to north of Lillehammer was now occupied by the enemy. Moreover, D Coy at Redalen and A Coy at Hellerud had heard the Lillehammer bridge go up in the small hours and knew what that meant. The importance of the bridges across the lake and the River Laagen which runs into it is obvious if considered from the point of view of General Ruge. He was fighting a delaying action in the hope that he would get more reinforcements from the British. His main forces were split down the centre by the great ditch that drains the

43

Gudbrandsdal valley. Already, the Norwegian position in front of Gjovik had been outflanked by a German advance across the mountains from the Randsfjord (Map 3). As he pulled back to where the valley narrows, his flanks were more or less protected by the snow-covered heights to east and west. The fourth prong of the German advance was many miles away eastwards in the Osterdal, driving north for Elverum (Map 1b), but the possession of the bridges was essential for contact between their own forces. When they were no longer tenable they had to be destroyed.

According to the Norwegians their available forces in the area on the east side of the River Laagen were disposed as follows:

One battalion of the 2nd Dragoons about and just south of Oyer and another battalion just north of Tretten. Dahl Force, to the West, had about three battalions on the road Frydenlund/Gausdal, in an area due west of Lillehammer; two battalions and two field battalions a short way up the tributary valley north-west of Faaberg and a battalion at the jink in the road two miles north of Gausdal. With Lillehammer bridge blown, the vital links remaining between General Hvinden Haug's and Col Dahl's forces were the road/river bridges at Faaberg (Map 5), the rail/river bridge at Hunderfossen (Map 6) and the road/river bridges at Oyer and Tretten. All these bridges were of lattice steel girder construction on piers. Rearguard to the main army of the Norwegians on both sides of the river were B and C Coys of the Foresters on the east with A and D of the Leicesters. On the west side of the lake were Foresters A and D Coys. B and C Coys of the Leicesters were still on their way from Aberdeen.

The new East Force position covered the river bridge at Faaberg as well as the main road north. Some civilian labour had been employed to prepare the site and Norwegian officers were available to indicate its features. But the delays described above prevented the British from reconnoitring; in addition, the troops arrived piecemeal in the small hours of the morning and had abandoned their signals and much other equipment for want of transport and petrol.

The late arrival of the Leicesters, tired, cold and hungry, had a very serious effect, as the new position south of the Balbergkamp (Map 3) had to be occupied by daylight, and the troops were pushed off into their positions by the brigadier as they arrived down the road. By this time, the Foresters and Leicesters were completely intermingled, making it extremely difficult for Battalion HQs to know where anyone was, and as all the signal equipment had to be abandoned, it was not possible to run a line out to the forward troops. The forest trees and the configuration of the ground made visual signalling impossible. It should be mentioned here that during the whole of the retirement cars and lorries were found abandoned by the roadside and the few with petrol in the tank and keys were quickly acquired to assist in transport. Altogether four cars and three

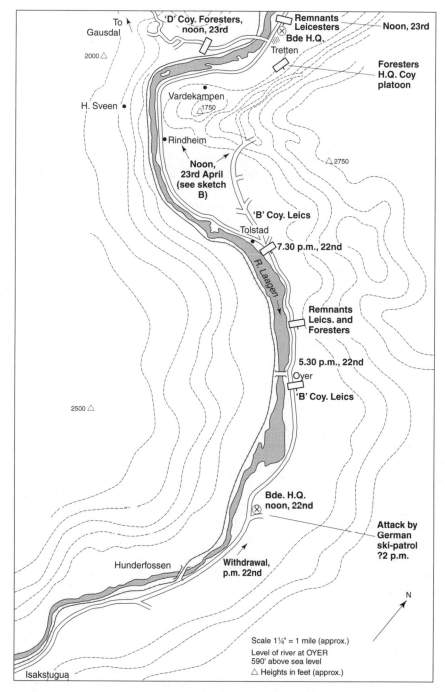

Map 6   Dispositions of 148 Brigade Tretten area 22/23 April.

lorries were appropriated by the battalion in this manner. Petrol, until the very end when pumps were exhausted, was always to be had for the taking by using those which had been abandoned by their owners.

The position was occupied by about 4.30 a.m. and the morning was spent by the Germans in reconnaissance by low flying aircraft, about which nothing could be done. OC C Coy, Redmayne, was met by the CO at a road junction just short of the Balbergkamp position. He reported the incident of the enemy motorcyclists at Brottum. The CO told him that two platoons of C Coy were up the hill on the left of the road, facing south and that the third was to be astride the road. There was a farm on the right around which B Coy was deployed. As a position it was not bad, for it covered the open ground down to the road from the edge of the woods, but there was no way of securing a field of fire through the trees to the south or to the east up the hill, so a standing patrol was placed in the trees above the forward position and they hoped for the best.

At about 11.00 a.m., the school, about half a mile north of the agricultural college, which sheltered the joint Battalion HQs, was machine-gunned from the air. The two COs went to brigade HQ, to report and ask for orders. They found that the brigadier had left for the north; they were ordered to wait for him at Oyer and accordingly set out on the road.

Col Dudley Clarke now appears somewhat unexpectedly on the scene. At Otta, halfway between Oyer and Aandalsnes, he had news at midnight of the collapse of the Lundehogda position and having a new and special assignment, which involved his retracing his steps southwards, came on to see what was happening. At about 1 p.m. that Monday at a crossroads beyond Oyer, he came across Brigadier Morgan with his two battalion commanders snatching a hasty luncheon on the verandah of a wayside Inn. They looked drawn and tired. Brigade HQ was without news of Major Roberts's two companies of Foresters on the advanced right flank. He learned of the new position now held on the Balbergkamp covering the road bridge across the river at Faaberg and there were hopes that the remnants of Roberts's men might join them there at any moment. They could have done with an extra two companies which would have made a difference to the troops on the east bank. While this was being explained to Col Clarke, a low-flying aircraft came up the road machine-gunning all and sundry and driving them hurriedly from the verandah into the dining room.

The brigade intelligence officer, Lt Thompson, 1/8 Foresters, was despatched to the Faaberg bridge in search of Roberts's party, but scarcely had he got away on a motorcycle before one of the battalion IOs drove up in a borrowed civilian car with an urgent message for his colonel. He said that the Germans had already begun to move round the

An aerial view of Otta.

flank and that another attack looked like starting at any moment. On that the meeting broke up and both COs hurried away to join their battalions. Events were hotting up.

We, the other half of the 1/5th Battalion of the Leicestershire Regiment which comprised B and C Companies and half of HQ Company, mainly the Transport and Bren-carrier Platoons, also a platoon of the 1/8 Battalion of the Sherwood Foresters who were mainly transport personnel like ourselves, arrived in Norway from Scotland, between 8 and 9 a.m. on 22 April 1940. Our arrival was monitored by a high-flying enemy recce plane as we staggered ashore. After one or two shots from our escorting destroyer HMS *Jackal* it flew off.

We drivers were somewhat despondent for we should have been driving our trucks and Bren carriers off the *Cedarbank* with all our equipment and supplies ready to drive wherever, but this was not to be.

After thirty-six hours on the storm-tossed ocean, we did not feel as though we wanted to drive very far in any direction and the *Cedarbank*, with all our supplies, was already at the bottom of the sea.

Soon after our arrival an enemy aircraft was still droning about overhead with no opposition except from the destroyer which had accompanied us down the fjord. The noise of the destroyer's guns reminded us that we were getting closer to the enemy. Before very long, we boarded a train together with what little food and supplies were available, and started off south towards Dombaas. The Norwegian trains had only hard wooden benches. The journey south to Dombaas took us from sea level to over three thousand feet where we travelled past huge snow-clad mountains, forests and a huge plateau covered in deep snow, before plunging down a twisted track towards Dombaas. We were helped on our way by one or two machine-gunning aircraft and we had to wait outside the town for about half an hour for there was an air raid in progress. One or two of us suffered cuts from the window glass which had shattered. I was lucky, I nose-dived under the opposite seat. Our platoon Sergeant, Dick Millington, was furious about this and deliberately set about priming a case of hand grenades showing us all how to do it for when the time came when we might have to.

By early afternoon our train had halted in Tretten station (Map 1b). The familiar wail of an air raid siren reminded us that we were at war. This was the first and the last air raid siren we were to hear in Norway. I trembled now, not so much at the cold, but at the thoughts of a face-to-face confrontation with the enemy. The fact that I would not be alone in this but would have my comrades beside me, did little to allay my fears.

My thoughts were abruptly terminated by the urgent shouts of officers and NCOs. I quickly found myself lumbered with our platoon's anti-tank rifle as well as my own rifle slung across my back.

'Come on, quickly, quickly,' shouted RQMS Halford running along to the next carriage. 'Leave everything on the train and get into the shelter of the trees.'

We staggered quickly from the carriages to the side of the track and into the forest and disappeared amongst the conifers. I came to rest in the shelter of a huge boulder, one of many which seemed to litter the edge of the trees.

After a few seconds, the roar of aircraft engines became audible and as I peered up into the sky my fingers tightened their grip on the smooth blue steel barrel of the anti-tank rifle. Every nerve in my body was as taut as the strings of a fiddle, not quite knowing what to expect. At the age of twenty-one I thought I was invincible and could put my fist through a door any time, but this was no door and would almost certainly fight back.

Like my comrades, the closest I had ever been to an enemy aircraft had been in the cinema back home. But this was no cinema – this was for real and curiosity made us all look upwards at the huge machine which suddenly appeared and roared over our heads in a kind of slow motion.

'Keep well under cover,' came a shouted order from somewhere amongst the trees, 'And do not give away our position by firing your rifles at it.'

The voice of Jim 'Nuffy' Hall, who was close to my boulder, identified the machine briefly.

'It's a Ju 88 bomber,' he said in a tone of voice which suggested it had no business to be here and Nuffy was usually right about most things. He didn't say much about anything, but when he did say something he was usually right.

'Naw,' Len Dunkley replied from the other side of the boulder, 'That's no bomber mate, or we'd all have been blown to kingdom come by now. I reckon its a recce plane and I'll bet he knows we're here and he's on his radio calling up the bloody Stukas.'

I forced myself to look up again at the evil black monster circling up above and found that my curiosity had evaporated leaving every nerve in my body taut and tingling with fear, expecting at any moment, regardless of Len's reassurances, to be blown away in the blast of a bomb. The machine was so low that I could see the pilot's head quite distinctly. The machine banked steeply over the station and turned away to the south, quickly disappearing from sight behind the hills. So we came to Tretten, a scattered little village beside the River Laagen which flowed south-east to join Lake Mjosa, close to the town of Lillehammer some twenty miles farther south.

Some of us from the MT and Bren-carrier Platoons made our way over the railway tracks towards some open ground close by Tretten bridge (Map 3).

Our Quartermaster, Lieutenant Morson, quickly made it known that the cooks were going to prepare us a hot meal of bully beef stew with the remains of the rations taken from the *St Magnus* and *Sunniva* at Aandalsnes. This was to be the first and last meal I and a good many of my comrades would get during the next ten days we spent in Norway.

Whilst we waited I relaxed as far as I could by removing my steel helmet and undoing my equipment belt and my greatcoat. Despite the fact the sun shone warmly my hands and feet were cold, but there was nothing I could do about it. I stood the anti-tank rifle against the bridge along with my Lee-Enfield rifle and removed the two fifty-bullet cloth bandoliers which were slung round my chest under my greatcoat and were quite heavy. I also had a meagre supply of 0.5 in rounds for the anti-tank rifle in my equipment pouches.

I lit a cigarette and looked around me and slowly began to take in and admire the surrounding scenery.

It was here that the valley narrowed into a gorge and on both sides the hills rose up to two thousand feet from the side of the road and the railway track on our side of the gorge. The station occupied a level piece of ground including the ground on which we sat by the bridge. The railway track continued on along a narrow ledge to Oslo via Lake Mjosa and Lillehammer (see photo).

Amongst the conifers on the hillsides the snow was knee deep. Across the river was a building which we came to know later as the cheese factory (Sketch B, page 51). This was also to become the cook house and later on the first aid post. There was very little that could be seen of the village.

Lillehammer and the bridge over Lake Mjosa.

Here and there amongst the trees on the hillsides could be seen one or
two timber-built houses so favoured by the Norwegians, but one had to
look for them to see them, so well concealed were they by the forest. Most
of them were empty, as we were to find later, the occupants having fled
from the advancing Germans. On the far side of the bridge, we could see
several cars, mostly American makes which as we found out later, had
been ditched by the side of the road, most of which bore evidence of
having been machine-gunned from the air. We could also see one or two
Norwegian army officers in their sky blue uniforms mingling with the
dark green uniforms of the rank and file. One or two officers came across
the bridge to confer with our own officers, but the most surprising thing
was that none of them, not even the rank and file, seemed to be wearing
steel helmets.

A kind of uneasy peace and quiet descended on us as we sat and ate

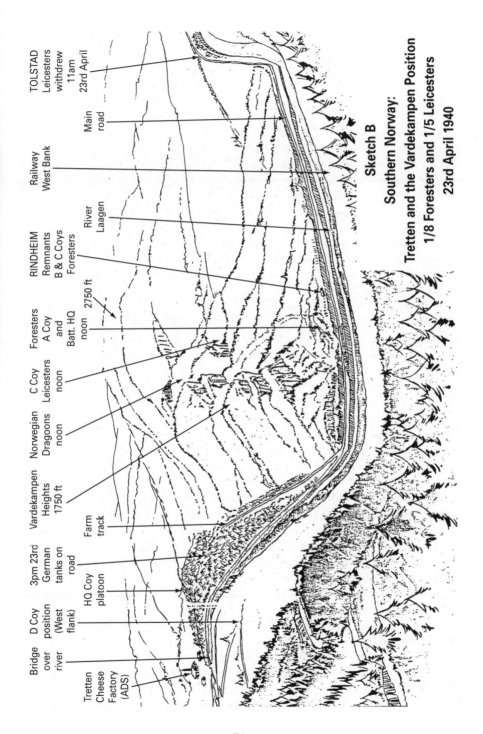

TOLSTAD
Leicesters
withdrew
11am
23rd April

Main
road

Railway
West Bank

River
Laagen

RINDHEIM
Remnants
B & C Coys
Foresters

2750 ft

Foresters
A Coy
and
Batt. HQ
noon

C Coy
Leicesters
noon

Norwegian
Dragoons
noon

Vardekampen
Heights
1750 ft

Farm
track

3pm 23rd
German
tanks on
road

HQ Coy
platoon

D Coy
position
(West
flank)

Bridge
over
river

Tretten
Cheese
Factory
(ADS)

Sketch B
Southern Norway:
Tretten and the Vardekampen Position
1/8 Foresters and 1/5 Leicesters
23rd April 1940

51

our bully beef stew, secure in the knowledge that the rest of our comrades of 148 Brigade were already with the Norwegians between us and the enemy.

As I washed out my mess tin in the waters of the River Laagen, I little realised that I would eat no more food for another ten days but the emergency ration sewed up in my battledress trousers and I would have to be really hungry to eat that because it tasted like a mixture of plain chocolate and gravy of the strongest kind.

The peace and quiet was not destined to last very long, but while it did, I took a closer look at this alien land that we had been sent to. What quirk of fate had led us into it with nothing more than a few small arms to stop the advance of a complete German army?

At the sound of approaching aircraft engines, confusion and shouting broke out on the other side of the gorge. Two or three truck loads of Norwegian troops who had arrived at the bridge spilled over the sides smartly and started firing their 0.28 in popgun rifles at the still distant enemy, before dashing for cover amongst the trees; some sheltered underneath the bridge. At the same time one or two more trucks, one of which appeared to be loaded with an ancient looking 75 mm gun complete with wooden wheels, arrived from the direction of Dombaas.

Amongst all this confusion, the voice of RSM Holyland was heard giving an order to the men of the Leicesters, who were still unloading supplies from the train.

'Anti-aircraft action – mount tripods,' he bellowed, and a very well drilled action saw some Bren guns mounted and preparing to fire at three Me 109 fighter aircraft which thundered up the gorge towards us, each one of them machine-gunning anything and everything. There was no warning air raid siren this time; it just happened.

There was confusion all around with shouted orders half drowned by the hellish din of the tree-hopping fighters and their machine-gun fire. Out of the corner of my eye I saw Norwegian troops fleeing before the onslaught into the shelter of the trees and the very thin veneer of discipline which I had somehow acquired during my short six months or so of service as a full-time soldier suddenly fell apart. It left in its place a terror-stricken inability to move a muscle in order to obey an overwhelming desire to run somewhere.

It was only the steadying voice of CSM Cleaver that saved us from our own folly.

'Geddown and lie flat,' he bawled and we dropped to the ground as one man.

Then came the bullets, snicking through the trees and kicking up little gouts of dirt inches away from where I lay and whanging in ricochet from rocky outcrops and boulders. I had a horrible feeling that I was the only target that the pilots could see and I felt as tall as the Statue of Liberty. I

Two views of Tretten bridge.

Joseph Kynoch with veteran Per Engh in Tretten station in 1999.

braced myself for the sudden impact of bullet against bone or the flesh-searing heat of the bomb that must explode beside me at any moment, but nothing of the sort happened. In a few seconds the machines had gone up the valley, leaving behind thunderous echoes so that once again out of the ensuing silence, we could hear the peaceful gurgle of the river as the waters flowed over its bedrocks. This time, one or two moans could be heard from comrades who had been hit by a bullet. This machine-gunning from the air was terrifying and morale destroying, because we knew that little could be done about it. Bren guns and rifles were of no use against 250 mph low flying aircraft.

A lone voice piped up from the silence amongst the men now struggling to their feet.

'Where the hell's the RAF?' it wanted to know. 'Why are they not here with us seeing to these bloody Jerries? Where are all our Spitfires and Hurricanes?' But no one answered his question. No one could.

A muffled crump brought us quickly back from the shock of our first taste of war as one of the aircraft dropped a 500lb bomb.

The most frightening aspect of the gorge at Tretten was the fact that any noise was magnified to an almost unbelievable pitch by the close proximity of the hills. It tended to bounce from one side to the other in a series of rumbling echoes.

Orders were again shouted, telling us to get ready to cross to the other side of the bridge and away from the vicinity of the railway station which it was said would become the target of the bombers before so very long.

B and C Companies were very quickly organised and sent across the bridge where a few Norwegian single-decker buses were waiting to take them on their way to join the rest of the battalion somewhere towards the town of Lillehammer. Corporal Arthur Thomas of C Company was prompted to remark, 'Fancy going into battle by bus!'

I found myself crossing the bridge with my anti-tank rifle across my shoulder with the rest of HQ Company to take up suitable defensive positions where it was thought there was a little less danger of becoming the victims of the low-flying aircraft. Corporal George Mee from Market Harborough and I were detailed by our platoon commander, Lt A.B. Speak, to get the anti-tank rifle set up and ready for action as soon as possible and to find a suitable site which commanded anything coming over the bridge from the direction of Gausdal (Map 3).

After searching an area facing the bridge, we selected a spot in a cutting in the rock which stood a little way back from the roadside and completely covered anything approaching from across the river.

Our instructions had been quite clear and any enemy tanks or armoured cars attempting to cross the bridge must be stopped.

'Have you ever fired one of these, Lofty?' George asked me.

'Yes,' I said, 'I fired it on the ranges back home and from what I remember there was a helluva bang and clouds of dust at the muzzle end.'

'Oh, I wouldn't know for I've had nothing to do with them.'

'Mind you, I don't know how the hell I'm supposed to stop a tank or even an armoured car with this, for it fires only half-inch bullets – not much bigger than a .303 rifle bullet, .197 to be precise, nearly two-tenths bigger, but still only a bullet. It needs an anti-tank gun to stop a tank, something like the 25 mm Hotchkiss that they've got in France.'

'Ah, but your half-inch bullets are supposed to be armour-piercing,' George replied. 'Anyway, I agree it would have to be a lucky shot to stop anything with them, but we shall soon find out, I'm sure.'

Further conversation was stopped abruptly by the sound of approaching aircraft engines belonging to the three Me 109s that had machine-gunned us a short time before.

'It's no good firing random shots at them as our comrades the Norwegians do,' shouted RQMS Halford, 'The best way is to get into line with a bullet up the spout and aim just ahead of the propeller and wait for the order to fire.' So we got into line, about twenty of us, Stan Pollard and his mate George Gough manned HQ's only Bren gun in the middle of the station yard across the river. We watched as the aircraft approached from the north. I still had an uncontrollable desire to disappear down the nearest rat-hole and as the three aircraft passed overhead, we let fly with our rifles, but nothing happened – then after a moment or two one of them began to trail a plume of black smoke behind it and the engine spluttered and coughed ominously. A cheer went up at this and it disappeared from view in a cloud of smoke. We heard later that it had crashed further south.

I suddenly began to feel homesick and to wonder if I would ever see home again. I soon began to discover that I was exhausted from lack of sleep and my stomach ached from its repeated efforts to empty itself into the sea the day before.

It must have been well into the afternoon on that day when Corporal Mee spotted two specks high up in the sky.

'I think we're going to get a pasting, Lofty,' he said as he looked down at me lying on the ground alongside the anti-tank rifle with my eyes glued to the far side of the bridge, half expecting an enemy tank to appear.

George was a very reliable type to be with, his unruffled outlook generally inspired a lot of confidence in whoever was with him, but no sooner were the words of warning out of his mouth when confused shouts broke out on all sides of 'Take cover', 'Get down' and 'Get into the trees'. It was all so confusing that it was not easy to know what to do and in the event we did nothing.

'Don't worry, Lofty, they're after the train, not us.' George never moved a muscle and I was frozen alongside my rifle.

I watched spellbound as the two specks dipped suddenly towards the gorge in a headlong dive, one behind the other, their sirens opening out into a scream. The scream became a bloodcurdling howl as they raced earthwards. We could now see that they were Stukas and that they were aiming for the station.

That old feeling of helpless panic swept over me again and I wanted to run blindly in any direction as the gorge suddenly erupted in what was to my mind nothing short of a volcano. The ground trembled with the force of the explosions as the bombs burst in the station and the Stukas pulled back up into the air. The explosions echoed and reverberated and columns of black smoke and flying debris filled the air. I watched the whole scene with a kind of mesmerised terror unable to move a muscle.

I looked round at George who still sat unperturbedly on a slab of rock rubbing his chin with his hand.

'Well, Lofty – that's the end of that,' he said nodding towards the station. 'That's one train that won't be going anywhere for a while and the only hope of getting out of here is either on a lorry or Shanks's pony, that is if we survive that long.'

No sooner had the sound of the Stukas vanished behind the hills than the sound of lorries coming from the direction of Lillehammer in the south took their place. In a little while two lorries stopped, loaded with Norwegian troops and one or two wounded Leicesters and Sherwood Foresters. We walked over to them curiously and listened to their stories.

'Gi's a fag mate,' one of them asked me, 'I'm dyin' fer a smoke.' I pulled out some cigarettes and offered one to him and a Norwegian soldier, who took one out of the packet with a friendly smile. The tales they told of the situation they had left behind poured out of them. A corporal of the Sherwood Foresters said:

> You can't see the Jerries for bleedin' trees, then before you can even cock your rifle, they're on top of you and they've all got automatic rifles that spray you with bullets. Some silly bastard wanted to dig trenches and put up barbed wire, can you imagine it? Jerry would have got round it, over it or through it with the kit he's got. Anyway it would have been impossible to dig trenches for the ground was frozen solid. Jerry's got the lot, even incendiary bombs that set the bloody trees on fire and you with them if you don't move sharpish. We tried to stop their tanks with tree trunks but they just shove them out of the way. Then every so often their aircraft come along machine-gunning and dropping the odd bomb. Then they mortared us and shelled us from their tanks – it's bloody hopeless trying to stop them with rifles and Bren guns – we might as well have peashooters, and the anti-tank rifle is a disgrace and the people responsible for buying this useless piece of equipment should be here with us showing us how to stop an enemy tank with it. At night it's cold and we might as well be in our birthday suits as in our own gear.

Another one spoke up:

> We had a couple of 3 in mortars with us which we set up to fire at an enemy machine-gun post which was pinning us down and when we fired the first two bombs off there was no explosion that you'd have expected, oh no, there was just this bloody cloud of smoke, we could almost hear the Jerry's laughing, honestly, Fred Carno's army just isn't in it.

The sudden sound of aircraft engines to the south of us had everyone craning nervously skywards to see what it was. The poor Norwegians looked haggard and drawn, but were cheerful enough, although they were absolutely terrified of aircraft, which was very understandable, for they petrified us. The sound of even a distant one was enough, and who could blame them for we little knew at the time that they had even less to defend themselves with than we had. I saw one of their cannon and that was an old 75 mm mounted on ancient wheels that looked as though it might have been used in the Napoleonic wars. The one thing they did have was the courage and the guts to try to halt the German advance and so far they had done well; but their efforts had not been good enough. They just did not have the men or the equipment necessary to stand up against the blitzkrieg, and in an hour or so this would be our own situation.

Neither the Norwegians nor ourselves had been trained in modern blitzkrieg warfare which the Germans had demonstrated so efficiently on the Polish plains only a few months before.

Here in Norway, it was a different kind of battleground from the European one, with deep snow and valleys hemmed in by steep snow-capped mountains on either side; but the blitzkrieg was the same. Stukas were used to demoralise, and the high-level bombers to prepare the way for the tanks and troops and their fighter aircraft to shoot up and bomb trains, lorries and troops. There were also Austrian ski troops on the mountains protecting the enemy's flanks, at the same time outflanking us. They also used paratroops. It was well known that they used troops wearing Norwegian uniforms and speaking the language to create confusion everywhere as they advanced northwards from Oslo.

They were so well equipped, and confident with it, that any resistance they met they simply bypassed, leaving in their wake confused pockets of troops who had to try and rejoin their units under the cover of darkness. Because it never got darker than a deep twilight, travelling by road was dangerous which meant a circuitous journey over the hills in deep snow. The alternatives were escape over the mountains to Sweden or simply sit still and be taken prisoner.

The aircraft which we had all been looking at so apprehensively in the distance turned out to be a transport plane on its way to Trondheim from Oslo, ferrying troops to reinforce their garrison there. The civilian drivers of the two lorries didn't wait to find out what it was, but let in their clutches with a jerk and disappeared up the road towards Dombaas.

Our platoon officer Lt Speak came over to where we had set up the anti-tank rifle.

'You'll have to manage this on your own now, corporal,' he said. 'I need Lofty here and a few more HQ personnel to make up a standing patrol up in the trees on the hillside to protect us from attack by enemy ski troops.

I never saw George again after that and have often wondered what became of him. I followed Speak down the road and in fifty yards or so came to a piece of open ground on the right-hand side going north. It was fairly flat and must have been an acre or two in extent, divided by a dry-stone wall about three foot high running at right angle from the road up to the treeline. Here I was handed over to Len Dunkley to make up the patrol to five men. Another patrol was in the charge of Corporal Alan Lord of the Bren-carrier Platoon. Before we could move off on patrol we were intercepted by Sergeant Dick Millington who relieved each of us of 90 rounds of ammunition leaving us with just ten rounds in our magazines.

'Sorry about this lads, but they're running out of ammunition up front and without it they'll never stop Jerry and we'll all end up prisoners of war or worse.'

After ridding ourselves of the heavy cloth bandoliers of bullets, we moved off towards the sloping, tree-clad hillsides in single file. 'Digging in' usually meant a hopeless struggle of spade against rock or solid frozen ground and defence had to consist of loose stone parapets or 'sangars'. We all wore our greatcoats over our battledress and our equipment on top of that but the cold still penetrated.

As we progressed through the deep snow up the hillside and between the conifers it was not easy to see more than a few yards ahead. We were all ravenous with hunger, for the little bit of stew we had at midday had long gone.

We had not gone far when the voice of Alan Lord, who was up front, shouted back that there was a house close by and he was going to ask them if they had anything to eat. They moved up towards the door and Alan gave it a few knocks and waited, but he needn't have bothered for the place was empty. Although we searched the place, there was not a crumb of food anywhere.

We carried on up the hill cursing the cold and the mini-avalanches of snow which occasionally fell from the upper branches. Before we had gone very far our trouser legs and boots were soaked and after a while we stopped for a breather and noticed that we were almost on a level with the hills on the other side of the gorge. At this time, enemy aircraft were very active flying up and down the valley machine-gunning the woods as well as the road. We moved on up towards the summit of the hills and as we got closer the trees began to thin out again, until very soon, we could see a treeless, snow-covered countryside extending as far as the eye could see.

'No wonder they have ski patrols,' Len Dunkley remarked, 'I reckon you'd need skis or snow shoes to get across that lot.'

The two corporals had a short discussion as to which direction the two patrols should take and after Len had tossed a coin and won the toss, we wished Alan good luck with his patrol to the south-east towards the enemy and hoped we'd see them when they returned later on. We never saw them again.

At this particular time, late afternoon on 22 April, the Germans were advancing on Tretten and were getting closer by the hour. Our comrades of 148 Brigade were being pushed back from Lillehammer by the sheer weight of armament both on the ground and in the air.

After our patrol parted from Alan Lord's in the hills above Tretten, we carried on north-west through the trees in extended order and almost parallel to the roadway through the valley.

It was late in the afternoon when two Me 110s began systematically machine-gunning the trees around us and we dropped to the ground, keeping as close to the trunks of the trees as possible. I listened horrified as the chatter of the guns was quickly followed by the sound of bullets snicking through the branches and the soft thud as they struck the snow covered ground was all that I could hear. I got the old feeling that I was the only target they could see and that they were only firing at me. I scrabbled in the snow with my hands, trying to keep as close to the tree trunk as possible. Then I felt a gentle sort of tug at my water bottle and then something wet trickling slowly down my leg and my whole body seemed to freeze and I remained frozen until the aircraft had gone, then the voice of Len Dunkley penetrated my brain.

'What's up, Lofty – you're not dead are you?'

'No but I – I think I've been hit,' I stammered, 'In the leg.'

'Well, I can't see any blood about, mate, but there's a helluva lot of water. I think your water bottle must be leaking.'

I stood up and took the bottle out of it's webbing sling and examined it.

'My God,' I spluttered, 'that was a close one,' I said, handing the bottle to Len. The bullet had sliced along the metal side of the bottle just deep enough to leave a slit through which the water had leaked through onto my trousers.

We continued our patrol through the trees and shortly came to another house. It was vacant like the other one. I was lucky, I found a pair of ski mittens which I put on my freezing hands. Although we searched the house from top to bottom there was nothing to eat, only a small piece of Norwegian black bread which had started to go mouldy and was as hard as concrete.

As dusk approached, we made our way slowly back down through the conifers, among which I felt most uneasy for some unknown reason, perhaps it was because they grew so closely together and could conceal the means of a sudden death in the form of the guns of enemy soldiers. There is nothing more frightening than the prospect of being a target for an unseen enemy.

Len decided that we should spend the few hours of darkness, or deep dusk, in the shelter of the old drystone wall where we might be able to get an hour or so of badly needed sleep.

As we lay down in our greatcoats on the snow, Len said he would keep watch for the first two hours. I was surprised to find I didn't feel tired so much as cold. I felt frozen. I couldn't feel my legs below my knees and my feet were completely dead. I lay looking up at the sky for a long time watching the pale white fingers of the aurora borealis moving from side to side across the sky above the mountain tops in the north. It had been a long day.

Farther to the south a platoon of the Leicesters led by Lt Gillies Shields was approaching Arneberg to give battle to the Germans. The road was blocked in places with fallen timber which became a mass of flame that spread from tree to tree and made an easy target for German field artillery and deadly mortar fire.

Lt Shields recollects that:

> For seven hours the battle raged around the Neverjells and then on orders to retire to higher ground, we slowly staged a planned withdrawal. The only way to climb the hill was by the road.
>
> This episode of our withdrawal will stay with me for the rest of my life. The four-inch (100 mm) mortars, were, I'm sure, the key to German victory, worth more to infantry for close support, than planes or guns.
>
> They got our range and as we climbed they raised their sights. We heard the mortars fire their bombs and timed our dives to ground before they whirred from out of the sky. We kept our heads until we reached the crest and made defences on the hill, but sad to say, in that long haul two of my men were killed and several more had wounds and could not walk. When we backed an ambulance down the hill to gather them, the barrage stilled for long enough to load them up.
>
> We drew our rations, sparse and cold and used our rum to warm our weary bones. Then orders came to move once more towards Aasmarka. We heard the groans of tanks not far away, the roar of engines stuck in snow and then, when on the march, the sudden zooms of fighter planes and saw the frozen surface of the road pop up plumes of ice. We fired our Brens and rifles at them and how we cheered when one was hit and spurted smoke and flames!
>
> I was met by the CO, Col German, and he told me to hurry back and whip in all the waverers for by six o'clock the bridge would be blown. We were to make for Faaberg ridge (Map 3), our new defensive line. I never saw the good and brave CO in that campaign again. He fought a futile war against all odds, was overrun, cut off and caught.
>
> I gathered up my weary flock and made them move. At six o'clock we heard a thunderous boom echo around the hills and knew our chance to cross the bridge had gone and as we went down towards the town we passed an ambulance and several lorries burning hard. One house stood out from the rest, for this one displayed a large red cross on its roof. We walked towards this house and saw a sight which gave us all the proof we needed to know that a German corps was in the town. A long convoy of open trucks in which sat men upright and stiff and grim. We then entered the hospital and sought for news of British troops. A tall and beaming orderly said he knew that all the town was German now and we should stay and wait for his return to bring us help and keep us free from harm. But soon a nurse came and warned us that the man had run to fetch the Huns. He was the Quisling number one of the town. I thanked this loyal nurse and asked if

she could find us food to take away with us. A trolley table with bread and cheese was then brought out and these were loaded in our packs. Her final act was then to scout outside and mark my map with tracks to take to reach the path that led to Mailhaugen, a mountain ski resort.

I found the men and fed them as best I could. By this time we had been joined by other Leicesters including two officers.

We made some tea in our mess tins and after drinking it, set off in files to find the mountain track.

We'd walked that day about twenty miles and found the mountain tough to climb. As we got near the top a bonny maid sat waiting in a rocky lair and handed Capt. Tony Cripps a note in English. It said, 'Follow this girl and she will lead you safely here.' The captain asked the girl who wrote the note, but he got no reply. He tried in German then in French but no response. He went ahead with her and said that when he blew his whistle loud and sent her back with map and gloves we'd know it was no trap. We waited till the signal came and down the snow the maiden slid and what a thrill it was to reach the sun-clad crown.

Norwegians, all in skiing gear, seemed to have forgotten there was a war going on and down the slopes they weaved in sheer exuberance.

An old man told us that most of them had been caught on holiday and did not dare to travel home. He then gave us some food and went to find a truck to take us further north. With luck we might catch up with our own troops. He soon returned with two old army trucks of doubtful age and power.

We drove across a wide plateau. Suddenly an aircraft whose sound we had not heard came round a peak. It circled round about a mile away then made a slow deliberate turn and roared towards us, all guns blazing. We thumped the driver's cab roof with our fists to bid him stop. In panic we tried to stride away with snow up to our hips, but flopped in waves of drifts and hid, we hoped, from harm.

The plane returned and with incendiary bullets, set alight the canvas hood of both trucks. As they burned, he flew away. We ran to rip the blazing canvas down and strip the seats already on fire. The drivers started up the engines and off we went again. Three more times the strafing plane returned to finish us off. In the last attack a petrol tank was hit and with a blast exploded in flame and cast us all into gloom. Now we had to squeeze the men into the one remaining truck and left our packs behind to gain the standing space required, and crawled to reach a high-standing hotel they called Nevra. Here we wondered why so many people skied and bore so little sympathy with their Norwegian brothers-in-arms. They gave us smorgasbord and beer and rooms in which to wash and shave and promised us a meal and beds to sleep on. I doubt if our men had ever seen such luxury before, or had such kindness showered on them. But soon we had to face unpleasant facts. We had deceived ourselves and really could not blame the crisis that arose upon our hosts. A Swedish colonel came to us. His face was pale and grave. He said that as officers we must behave and act with honour and not shed civilian blood. If we stayed in Nevra, Germans would release their bombs upon the place and he prayed that we would leave. It was quite true that Nevra was a holiday resort with many children there. We knew now we had to go without delay. He said we ought to proceed north about six miles and move into some mountain huts which he thought were beyond the reach of German ski patrols. He would provide us with a guide to take us there and who would see what else we might require. We tied supplies on sledges. Our destination was Hundersetter.

When looking back I can recall five years of war, all overseas, but this was the very worst of all the marches that I had made. Burmese campaigns were cruel and tough, Somaliland was hot and dry and Abyssinia was very rough, but none of these campaigns tested my strength and will as did the snow of Norway.

And when we reached the huts at last we were so tired we could not taste the salted fish or any of the rich repast the Nevra chef had packed for us. We ticked off names as men went by the gate. Exhausted, cold but not downcast, each man was allocated a hut to share. We gave them tea and made them change their socks. All but a few reported in and aid was sought from guides who later found the stragglers and brought them in.

The whole rollcall complete, we went inside to light the stove. Next day, it snowed without a break and we were pleased the wind had swept our tracks away. We asked our guide to find us skis. But we dare not go out by day at all, as planes were regularly overhead. When the moon came up we learned in style to ride the slopes and very soon became quite good. We went a mile uphill one night to test the skis. We had the best instruction possible in time of war from four Norwegian men and Colonel Jansen. He told us that the Germans had just shot some civilians who had tried to hide an Englishman. We knew the tide had turned. That night, we lined up all the men and skied about ten miles. We got to Skollasetter, where we had been told was food.

When we got there we found not a thing to eat. We brewed the tea we brought with us and lay inside the huts a while to rest and wax our skis and plan the way we should go, north, east or west. The quest for food was critical. Our map revealed the next homestead would take at least a night of travelling without mishap – and would there be food? For the sake of safety, we thought it would be wiser to retrace our tracks. When we rolled up at our base, we found that the huts had been acquired by the Sherwood Foresters of our brigade.

We called our last parade next day at dawn and told the men they must divide themselves by midday into small self-chosen groups of four or five. We would then share with them all sufficient food to stay alive for several days.

At night we'd tell each group to make a break on every hour and dash for cover of the trees. We said that disguise of any sort would be very foolish for the Germans would shoot such people as spies if they were caught. The men were also advised it would be best to keep off roads and steer clear of towns and if they could not reach our troops up north, they must steer a course due east for Sweden.

The officers were last to go in two groups. We then all said farewell to the guides, Jansen and the three Norwegian girls who brought us food each night at risk to themselves of being shot. The snow was falling fast; our pace was brisk as we departed, keen to show we were not beaten yet, and so a trek of fourteen days began towards the north. Some nights we'd break our rule and make a call on valley farms and ask for food. But on the whole, we found our food in the summer farms. We stole the hams and cheese. We stole to live and lived to eat. Our desperate craving for food and rest released a latent force within us to drive us through the barrier of pain and hunger.

We crossed a white plateau one day into the wind and sun. The glare reflected from the snow affected me badly and I was left behind next day with snowblindness and had to lie for several days supine and in darkness. A fine Fenrick (2nd Lt) by the name of Erik von Krogh, was there with some Norwegian troops and they were very kind to me. I swear he saved my sight. One stormy day, he skied to Ringebu to find a chemist's shop but found the town in German hands. He hid behind a barn until the sun went down, then like a thief, he slunk and crept round the streets until he found a pharmacy. Von Krogh told his tale and stressed how much these desperate deeds must never be revealed. The brave Fenrick returned in blinding snow with cocaine drops. I know he travelled thirteen miles that night on skis and risked his life for me and thanks to him my normal sight was soon restored. This group of Norwegians who were helping to look after me were part of No. 2 Oppland, a cavalry-ski troop of some eighty men cut off from their squadron and now prepared to move up north. Their medical officer nursed and cared for me. His name was Humerfeld, a name I will never forget. Within a week the fates ordained to change my luck and perk me up no end. I heard a shout outside and saw my friends were there. This was a surprise to me for we had agreed that if one fell out the others would go on and waste no time on one who could not keep up with the rest. Apparently, the group had done their best to reach our troops north-west of Dombaas when they heard that all the British force had been got out of Norway safely. On hearing of this withdrawal, they had turned about. Our Colonel and CO Guy German had been caught by the enemy and three of our best friends had been killed and most of our regiment had not made the voyage home.

We went on our way to Sweden very much afraid that we might yet be captured. By day we slept, at night we skied and had our moments of despair, of fun and occasional rows. Near Hanstead, we found Reg Coleman the battalion IO and a guide who helped to plan our route ahead. There was no longer a need to hide by day, the country was so bleak and bare, which made our food more hard to find. It took a week to trek the hundred miles before we reached the Swedish line where we were interned for several months. Then one day we were sent to Finland and then across the sea to England and our regiment.

FOUR

THE NORWEGIANS WITHDRAW

B y Sunday, 21 April, things began to warm up. During the morning the two companies of the Leicesters A and D moved up, being attacked from the air on the road but without casualties, to the Aasmarka area; here they were immediately plunged into the difficulties of the terrain. Digging-in was impossible due to the frozen ground and sangars were built with stones and boulders to provide some shelter from bullet and shell splinter, but these would not have held off an attack. The Norwegian posts were on a freezing hillside about twelve hundred feet above sea level and based on a few small farm buildings, but stretching as far as the eye could see were thick conifer woods on all sides, covered in some three feet of snow. The Germans were already firing on the position with artillery and mortars from a range of about 3,000 yards and the arrival of the two companies of the Leicesters under Lt Col Guy German was also followed by an almost immediate increase in the rate of mortar fire and by attacks through the woods on both flanks. Col German was requested by the Norwegian Dragoons commander, Col Jensen to take over the whole divisional front. Col German objected. How could his 400 men replace 1,000 Norwegians? Instead, he selected a position south of Aasmarka and astride the main road. Here A and D Coys of the Leicesters prepared their first position, settled in and waited. They didn't have to wait long, for at about 3 p.m., a party of Norwegians carrying a large white flag came through their positions. These proved to be the first of the Norwegian forward troops pulling out and it was not long before 148 Brigade, on the east side of Lake Mjosa, consisting of two companies of the Sherwood Foresters B and C and two Coys of the Leicesters A and D, found itself left to cover the withdrawal of the major part of the Norwegian army to positions between twenty and thirty miles to the rear.

To the scorn of the Norwegians, the British troops appeared to be unable to leave the road, the only place where the snow was firm underfoot, simply because their clothing was unsuitable for deep snow, especially their footwear. The brigade then withdrew behind Aasmarka, immediately south of Lillehammer, where the road could be held in depth. This proved to be the first of many fighting withdrawals in which the brigade was last to leave. This slowly but inevitably reduced its

Lt Col German with Norwegian Lt Henrik Broch and Captain Ford-Smith leaving
Tretten station.

numbers and sapped its strength in the bitter cold of a Norwegian spring.

By about 8 p.m. the Dragoons had withdrawn from both their front
and reserve lines, through the new British position and had retired northwards as planned but the plight of the British troops had not gone
unnoticed by Col Jensen the Dragoons Commander who passed a
comment which summed up the whole situation.

'A difficult job in a strange land,' he said, 'In frost and snow and dark
thick forest on all sides. It is difficult enough for us who are used to these
conditions, but for them it must be sheer hell.'

Platoon Sergeant Major John Shepphard of the Leicesters HQ Coy
mortar platoon gives his own version of events.

> We realised that the Germans were stepping up the rate of mortar fire and
> were beginning to attack through the forest, also there appeared to be a
> troop of about four guns some two thousand yards away from us with a
> calibre of almost 150mm. Of course our mortars, which were 3 in, only
> had a range of some 1,600 yards and we didn't appear to have any bombs
> for them other than smoke, but we fired them off nonetheless from one
> mortar. The other mortar we discovered had no base plate and so was
> virtually useless. The fact that we had nothing but smoke bombs and only
> one base plate was probably due to the chaos of loading and unloading our
> stores from one ship to another at Rosyth. We had no signal equipment

67

and so all our communications had to be by runner and there was no guarantee that he would get there or back again through the trees with any messages. Sometimes figures would appear at the edge of the trees. Were they men of another platoon? Were they our allies the Norwegians or were they the Germans? We had no way of knowing without field glasses.

Of course, we were also obliged to use the natural cover of the trees which were very soon to be set on fire by incendiary bombs from the enemy mortars and we could only hold our position for a short time before we had to move back in the face of cannon fire.

Disengaging from the enemy, especially a victorious and advancing one, is no easy matter. The fact that the Leicesters did so under such difficult conditions of thigh-deep snow and bitter winds and under continuous pressure, reflects the greatest credit on all who took part in these battles. PSM Rowlinson, in this first disengagement, though badly wounded and with only an improvised platoon, so inspired his men that they played a very important part in the success of the operation. Occupying a post that was the key to the whole position, he continued to hold on until overrun and during this time succeeded in inflicting the greatest possible casualties on the enemy, for which he was awarded the Norwegian Military Cross.

The second withdrawal was to follow almost immediately, for as soon as the remainder of the two companies arrived at Aasmarka, a message

Platoon of D Coy Leicesters leaving Tretten station for the front.

was received that they were to continue their withdrawal to Faaberg, a village a mile or so north of Lillehammer.

PSM Shepphard marched back up the road with his platoon in good order, to our transport behind us. As we withdrew the Germans kept up their shell fire. Then we had orders to defend a valley to the south of Lillehammer and we took up a position behind some rocks. We had to snatch an hour or two of sleep whenever we could. Then we discovered that Austrian ski troops had got behind us and we had to move back yet again. It was more like a battalion exercise back home but for the shells and the bullets and the machine-gunning aircraft which were very demoralising.

We marched back up the road again and came to a kind of sunken road on one side where it looked as though a Norwegian artillery battery had been located. They had been caught by German shells. It was a scene of utter carnage. The roads were all unmetalled and made up of rolled stone and soil and were so narrow that two vehicles could only just pass.

This second withdrawal, which endangered the positions of the Sherwood Foresters on the other side of the lake, now necessitated a definite time limit for troops retiring from Aasmarka to avoid being trapped by the enemy. Norwegian transport was scheduled to pick them up by 1 a.m. next morning, 22 April. But no transport materialised and the Leicesters set out to march the twenty miles to reach Faaberg (Map 3), if possible before light.

PSM Shepphard and his platoon reached Lillehammer and came into the town in a civilian lorry just as a German armoured column was leaving in the opposite direction. 'We went into a big hotel for we were all ravenously hungry by this time and we were given tea and a couple of rock cakes each. Most of us had something to eat.'

The rest of the Leicesters under Col German who had set out to march to Faaberg eventually arrived well after daylight and after a long detour through the deep snow on the hills and the dark conifer forest. Here, many were found to be missing including OC A Coy Captain Cripps, Lieutenants Astbury, Savage, Scott, Shields and the warlike medical officer, Lieutenant Gorrie, also a complete platoon of D Coy. The story is best told in the words of Captain Cripps.

> Eventually, we reached Lillehammer and went into action with A Coy. This wasn't too easy as the Norwegians whom we were relieving left as we arrived. The snow was deep and it was very difficult to pass each other. It was about this time that we discovered that our only 3 in. mortar ammunition was smoke which was no help to us and the night before I had noticed that the only map available to us was on too large a scale to be any good. We stayed in position that day but the next night we had orders to withdraw. D Coy did so successfully except for the rearguard platoon,

which stayed behind until the appointed time and then retired to find that the local transport had left and so the troops had to march. This platoon with some of HQ Company, picked up a few stragglers and then managed to get one lorry load through and back to the battalion. Another platoon, mainly without any more ammunition, except for a few revolver rounds, marched on through the night. By some quirk of chance, this platoon took a left fork about midnight and arrived in Lillehammer about 8 a.m. the following morning. A German force, about ten minutes after midnight took the opposite right hand fork and reached Lillehammer rather earlier. When this rearguard platoon tried to get a wash and something to eat at a small hotel, the proprietor regretfully refused for he had been warned to offer greater facilities to the German HQ.

In view of their lack of ammunition, this platoon of D Coy took to the mountains and spent about ten days trying to get ahead of the Germans and so rejoin the Leicesters, but by this time the battalion had withdrawn from Norway and found that they had no alternative but to make their way over the mountains to Sweden.

On Sunday 21 April, Brigadier Morgan and Col Dudley Clarke attended a conference at Norwegian GHQ at Oyer called for 4 p.m.

When they entered Norwegian Headquarters it was obvious that something had gone seriously wrong and General Ruge told them that German tanks and reinforcements had been pouring into Oslo during the past few days and that he expected a renewed attack at any moment. He was proposing to withdraw his tired-out troops some twenty to thirty miles back up the valley. This plan had already started to operate and he pointed out that unless substantial British troop and equipment reinforcements arrived soon, they would face a critical situation. He asked that Colonel Clarke return at once to London and personally lay his request before the CIGS. This was at once agreed.

In the words of Brigadier Morgan:

> There was no need to enlarge upon the dangers facing the one and a half British battalions. Apart from the sudden prospect of being attacked in the very act of taking over and by tanks and howitzers, not to speak of the Luftwaffe against which we had virtually no defence, none of us had ever visualised them fighting almost alone without the main bulk of the Norwegian army.

The brigadier had certainly been posed a problem and he was still under Norwegian orders.

At about 12.30 a.m. on the night of 21/22 April, Captain Branston of the Sherwood Foresters met the Leicesters' IO, Captain Coleman at Slagbrenna crossroads (Map 4). The IO reported that as no transport had come to pick them up as was arranged, the two companies of his Battalion were marching from Aasmarka some seven miles farther south.

At about 2 a.m. the Leicesters arrived at Slagbrenna in a not very good mood. Captain Symington, OC D Coy stated that according to his orders, the Norwegian ski troops were to have held their position until 3 a.m. but had left two hours earlier. There was nothing now between them and the enemy and their transport had failed to turn up so they had decided to march back. Here I would like to quote a short account by Private D Murfet, Leicesters D Coy ration storeman, which goes some way to illustrate the confusion which arose between the British and Norwegian forces.

> The next day, some vehicles arrived to take us to join up with the Norwegians who were in contact with the Germans. There was not enough transport for about a dozen of us and our Corporal Hamer was put in charge with orders that we should march until we met up with them again. This we never did, for after an hour or so we came to a road junction and saw a large house about 100 yards up a drive and it was decided that we should stay there for the night.
>
> We could hear firing in the distance but this did not stop all except Hamer and myself, going to sleep. I was rather concerned especially when I heard vehicles on the road, so I went out to have a look. They were lorries loaded with troops and they were 'haring' down the road we had just come up. I went back to Hamer and told him what I had just seen and that I thought we should be out on the road. There was a lull in the traffic when we all got back down to the road and the others turned 'bolshie' and went back to the house. Shortly afterwards, another well loaded lorry dashed past and it was followed by an empty one driven by a Sherwood Forester, which I stopped. After explaining the situation to him, his reply was that he was sure that his was the last vehicle and he intended to move off at once and I could get aboard if I wanted to but he made it clear that he wasn't prepared to wait. I went back to the house and told Hamer what had happened and we all got back down to the road and as luck would have it, another lorry came along and we all got away.

As a matter of interest it should be mentioned that on this particular day, 22 April, several battles occurred at various places in the process of withdrawing and fighting rearguard actions in the area south of Lillehammer. One such action is described by Private G. Glenn of the Leicesters.

> I was with a group of HQ Company engaging the Germans when enemy aircraft came over and bombed a school. About twenty Norwegian children between the ages of six and ten ran into the trees for shelter. Then

the aircraft dropped bombs in the trees and the children ran out again and were caught in the cross fire between ourselves and the enemy. We withheld our fire, but the Germans carried on with their sub machine-guns. Most of the children fell, either killed or wounded and it was impossible for us to attempt anything in the nature of a rescue. I also saw a number of my comrades killed and wounded who were collected by stretcher bearers and taken to a local hospital. I also saw Private Coleman of Loughborough wounded. He had an eye blown out by the blast of a bomb and we took him onto the roadway, where he was picked up and taken to hospital. At that time we were fighting in groups; our group was Capt. Phillip Symington, Corporal Hamer, Privates Twigg, Murfett, and Blackwell.

Private Glenn was blown against a tree by the blast of a bomb and injured his back but he was only in hospital for a day.

It is not easy all these years after the event to piece together the fragments of information from a number of sources and make an attempt to build up an accurate picture of these few hours of an April afternoon in 1940 in a strange land.

At this particular time Brigade HQ was established at the crossroads just south of Oyer. Sentries had been posted at each side and the rear approaches to the HQ. Brigadier Morgan made it plain that the slopes on each side were giving him cause for anxiety. He had asked the Norwegians to send ski patrols along the ridges to stop any Austrian ski troops from working their way round. But so far, the patrols had made no appearance and until they did so Brigade HQ was in danger. One of HQ staff said:

It was one of the sentries at the back who presently called our attention to the mountain top, where the distant figures of skiers were now appearing. At first we thought they were the promised Norwegian patrols, then somebody shouted that they were bringing a machine-gun into position. A minute or two later it opened up and to our dismay we saw it was firing into the rear of the Leicesters' position. Behind the machine-gun more small figures appeared over the crest, then paused for a moment as though to regain their breath after a climb, then they hopped round to point downhill, then gave a push off with their ski sticks and came hurtling down the hill straight for us. There was only one thing to do then and that was to get out quickly while the Brigade HQ single Bren gun did its best to delay the onslaught. The handful of remaining troops were sent at the double up the road to the north, while the intelligence summaries and secret documents were set on fire. The brigadier, with what remained of his staff, made a hasty getaway by car in the direction of Oyer. Unfortunately, the Germans salvaged most of the papers which were unburnt and later on Dr Goebbels went to town on this scoop and made sure that the remaining neutral countries heard about it.

That afternoon of 22 April, the Leicesters withdrew again under constant aerial machine-gunning and bombing to just north of Oyer (Map 6). The attempt to hold the river crossing between Faaberg and the Balbergkamp had collapsed even before the half battalion of the Leicesters and Foresters had got into position and the cold, hungry and exhausted troops had no other alternative but to withdraw. Oyer was about half a mile behind them and here there was a good position free from trees and with a good field of fire, where they might make a stand. The men had lost all hope of stopping the enemy but they obeyed orders wearily.

Col German got them all into position once more but unfortunately they were then heavily bombed, as they dismounted from the vehicles which had brought them there. Two sticks of bombs fell amongst them and although they caused little damage and only a few casualties, the effect on the rest of the troops was critical and the only thing that prevented complete panic was the arrival of B and C Companies of the Leicesters from Aberdeen under the 2IC Major Atkins.

Bewildered stragglers were coming in now from left and right through the trees, while private cars drove past with their owners at the wheel, carrying British wounded to the civil doctors. In the midst of all this, lorry columns, still acting on orders of the previous night, were streaming back to the reserve area with the Norwegian regiments which had been relieved before the original attack had started.

It was very plain that they had no idea of the existing situation for they cheered happily at the sight of what they thought were fresh British troops coming in the opposite direction to join the battle. These highly welcome new arrivals were the last two companies of the Leicesters and no sooner had they dismounted from their gaily coloured buses on which they had scrawled 'Joy tours of beautiful Norway' than they were heavily machine-gunned by roving 109s. They had no experience of this kind of warfare, or for that matter any other kind of warfare. These young Territorials, who were clerks and shop assistants, farm lads and milkmen, were not so many days ago in England.

The Balbergkamp position was to have been held for twenty-four hours but the Germans planned otherwise and had the means to enforce it. The British troops who got back on the civilian lorries were largely without their company commanders. Six officers of the Leicesters had been cut off in Lillehammer. There had been no time for reconnaissance by OC companies in the rapid series of withdrawals.

As Norman Barnett of the Leicesters HQ Coy Signals platoon said afterwards:

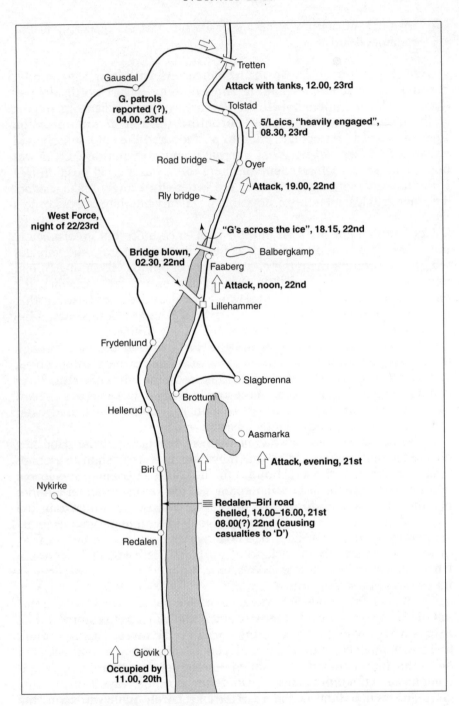

Map 7   The Gausdal Road, Nykirke to Tretten.

The Balbergkampen.

There was no communication within or between battalions except by runner and there were very few features to direct a runner by and there was always the chance that he would get lost, captured or even shot. There was no means of checking whether the message got through even, unless the runner returned.

In the platoon positions, officers and men had little food or sleep and if they had left the road at all, their feet and legs were almost certainly soaked and stiff with cold, leaving them open to frostbite. Sometimes figures would appear at the edge of the trees, were they men of another platoon? The Norwegians? The Germans? What was going on in the cover of the trees? Send a patrol up and the commander had only his compass to guide him back.

Sunday 21 April

We must now return to West Force for that day's activities. The half battalion had spent the night at Hellerud. Reveille was at 5 a.m. Col Dahl had rung up during the night and said that he wanted his rearguard company in position on the Stokeroen by noon. Accordingly, Major Roberts set off south again to inspect the position. South of Biri, the Germans occupied the east shore of the lake, barely 1,500 yards from the west shore road and meanwhile both companies of the Foresters were deployed. D were placed on the left and A on the right of the road. At 9 a.m. D Coy left Hellerud for Redalen where, owing to enemy air activity, it debussed and moved up on foot. The company was in position by noon. Here they had visitors, Brigadier Morgan, Col Dudley Clarke and Major Dowson, who had previously seen A Coy finishing work on their own posts before tackling the interrupted work in D Coy area down towards the lake. As they drove down by the lakeside road, a continual stream of Ju 52s was flying low up the far side, carrying supplies and reinforcements to the isolated garrison at Trondheim. The visitors soon returned to Lillehammer. At 2 p.m., with Major Broch commanding the left forward battalion of Dahl Force, (he was killed a few days afterwards) Major Roberts went to Biri for orders, their cars being shelled from across the lake on the way there.

Col Dahl told them that withdrawal of Dahl Force would begin as soon as darkness fell and that Major Broch, with the rearmost battalion, would inform OC D Coy (Major Kirkland) when the last Norwegians were clear and that OC D would then order the bridge over the Stokeroen to be blown. It was thought that this should be about 5 p.m. Other bridges were being prepared for demolition along the road. D Coy would hold on at the Stokeroen for one hour and then withdraw to Frydenlund through A Coy at Hellerud. General Ruge and Col King-Salter joined them while the conference was taking place.

At 5 p.m., Roberts, back on the Stokeroen, was giving Kirkland his orders. He then returned to Hellerud where, at 7.30 p.m. A Coy was given similar orders to D Coy: to drop the roadblock of tree trunks as soon as D Coy was clear next morning, hold on for one hour and then withdraw to Frydenlund. So A and half of HQ Coy were to occupy A's and D's positions. Major Roberts then left for Frydenlund. it was a bright moonlit night but the cold was bitter and penetrating.

The baggage party under Lt Sketchley again set out after dark to transfer the remainder of the unessential kit to Faaberg station. To do this, they had to cross the bridge at Lillehammer on the way to the station. On their return journey they looked in on Battalion HQ in the Victoria Hotel, but were informed by the Norwegian staff that they had left. The Germans were in fact, in the town a few hours later. 'We never saw our baggage again.' Sketchley said afterwards.

At 8 p.m. that Sunday, 21 April, A Coy at Hellerud got its first and last issue of food. At 11.30 p.m., rations were taken up to D Coy on the Stokeroen River in front of Redalen, at this time frozen solid, by the West Force MO Capt. Stoker.

'A' Company Capt. Beckwith reported that during the day enemy planes had flown over the position at about 3 p.m. and again at about 4 p.m. On both occasions the positions had been machine-gunned and bombed. On the second visit one of the planes was shot down. At that moment across the lake, almost due east of A Coy at Hellerud, B and C Coys Foresters and A and D Leicesters were in position ready to take over the rearguard from the 2nd Norwegian Division already withdrawing from Lundehogda and Arneberg (Map 3) but West Force knew nothing of all that.

The whole of the Norwegian Dahl Group had necessarily to move back when the retreat began on the east bank, and thereby lose contact with the Norwegian 4th Brigade still further west, because German artillery on the road between Lundehogda and Lillehammer could command the Biri/Lillehammer road and the Germans could also have crossed the ice. The Dahl Group, like the 2nd Division, employed the British detachment as its rearguard. The large bridge over the lake at Lillehammer had by this time been blown up.

Throughout the whole of the night of 21/22 April, Dahl Force was passing through the Hellerud position; their rearguard elements were clear of the Stokeroen by 5 a.m., when orders were given by OC D Coy, Major Kirkland, to blow the bridge. Major Kirkland had been given the 'all clear' by the Norwegian battalion commander, Major Broch.

The Norwegian engineers felled prepared trees across the road all the way back to Redalen. At 6 a.m. D Coy pulled out and withdrew northwards as ordered. There had been no sign of the enemy. Buses were waiting at the outskirts of the village (Redalen), 18 Platoon got into the first, 16 Platoon into the second, CQMS Cleary into the third with the ammunition, Major Kirkland and Lt J. Esam in a car and 2nd Lt Dowson with 17 Platoon in an open truck.

The first seven miles were uneventful when suddenly, on turning a sharp bend in the road, heavy mortar fire was encountered coming from the other side of the lake. Immediately all the drivers accelerated and shot through the danger area. The first two platoons and the ammunition truck got through without any casualties. The 17 Platoon truck unfortunately received a direct hit, killing the civilian Norwegian driver and five men and wounding three others. The wounded were taken to Lillehammer Hospital.

Hearing the explosions, OC Coy had immediately returned to deal with 17 Platoon and before continuing north had seen the wounded being attended to in a Norwegian dressing station.

By 9 a.m. the last of D Coy had passed through A's position at Hellerud, making for Frydenlund. This was to be the third British rearguard position.

At Hellerud, A Coy was waiting somewhat anxiously for the appearance of D Coy. It is perhaps worth while stressing here the effects of the lack of any means of communication. All that A Coy knew was that D Coy, some fifteen miles to the south of them, had been given orders to withdraw one hour after the last of the Norwegians were over the

77

Stokeroen. Having no adequate map, OC A Coy did not know the run of the roads or exactly where D Coy was, although it was true that A Coy had passed through Redalen two days before, on the way back from Nykirke. This lack of communication with D Coy meant that if they were attacked or bypassed by the enemy A Coy would know nothing of it until they themselves were attacked. Apart from the risk of an attack in the darkness over the ice on the lake to their left, which looked and undoubtedly was, thick enough to bear troops, A Coy had heard Lillehammer bridge go up in the small hours and guessed that, east of the lake, the Germans must be well behind them. To their unguarded right the forest rose steeply upwards to over 2,000 feet. Major Roberts, commanding West Force, had gone off early to Frydenlund to await D Coy.

At about 8 a.m. the buses carrying 16 and 18 Platoons and the ammunition truck swung into sight around a bend in the road. The passengers told of the shelling and said that Major Kirkland was behind, seeing to the wounded.

The bridge in front of A Coy's position, which the Norwegians had promised to mine, hadn't been touched and OC A was more than a little concerned about how long he could hold a two-company front with A Coy and the forty-six riflemen which were half of HQ Coy specialist platoons.

At 10 o'clock OC A Coy was up at the timber stack, with the Norwegian interpreter Jepson, ready to drop the roadblock, when round the corner trotted a shaggy pony drawing a sleigh. In it was a Norwegian soldier. He told Jepson that there were more behind. He seemed quite unconcerned about the war and hadn't seen any Germans. In the circumstances, they were allowed to pass. There were about thirty men in all, in thirty sleighs and they seemed to be in no hurry.

At about 10.30 a.m. the stack of tree trunks was somehow cascaded onto the road, and A and half HQ Coy embussed and by noon they had rejoined D at Frydenlund.

In the new position, D Coy was allotted to the right sector and A Coy to the left, with one platoon facing northwards in case of trouble from the Lillehammer direction. Due to the position having been partially dug by the Norwegians, the first task was given to the siting of Bren guns and the anti-tank rifles, wiring the bridge for demolition and the construction of a roadblock on the causeway leading from the bridge to the high ground. The bridge was blown at approximately 2 p.m. after the Norwegian engineers and some transport had passed over.

This position was a strong one and it was believed that a stand would be made. This was welcomed as everyone was extremely tired due to the continual movements and the taking up of successive positions day and night. There was an eagerness to get to grips with the enemy. All that afternoon, West Force was troubled by aircraft and constantly running for shelter.

At 6 p.m. telephoned instructions were received by major Roberts ordering West Force to withdraw from Frydenlund forthwith and go to Gausdal via the mountain road. OC A Coy, down on the lakeside road and nearly a mile from force HQ up the hill, eventually received orders to prepare to withdraw on D Coy. Shortly afterwards A Coy moved platoon by platoon and actually reached the rendezvous just ahead of time, only to find that everyone had gone on up the road. It was getting dusk. We plodded on up the hill and very soon ran into the rest of the force already embussed and waiting. Up to now there had been no signs of Germans. There seemed to be no vehicles left for A Coy. We finally pushed the company in on top of the already filled trucks and busloads. OC Coy and his batman walked on up the slowly moving column and managed to squeeze in beside the Norwegian driver and mate of a truck. The only orders had been to close up on D Coy. We had got pretty warm climbing the hill and the men had no greatcoats with them. As we got further up the mountain road, the moon rose beyond the lake and the air began to get more chilly.

The column moved off at about 10.30 p.m. About an hour later there was a long wait in an endeavour to pass the motor transport of a Norwegian battalion in the narrow roadway. Here, a valuable hour was wasted trying to find the Norwegian drivers, who had gone off to rest, taking with them their ignition keys.

The column was now well up above the tree line; until then nothing much could be seen but the column ahead. The Norwegian drivers spoke no English and in spite of the long halts, preferred not to stop their engines.

D Coy, who were in the lead, arrived at West Gausdal (Map 3) at about 2 a.m. It was hoped that a rest would be obtained at this secluded place in the mountains. The local priest had most kindly placed his church at our disposal. D Coy was actually bedded down for the night when, shortly after our arrival, fresh orders were received. These directed that West Force was to join its own brigade on the east side of the valley at Tretten where it was to go. Furthermore, it was intimated that enemy patrols were already in the outskirts of West Gausdal. D Coy was roused and the vehicles loaded. While the front half of the convoy may have reached Gausdal around 2 a.m., the rear half had not. OC A Coy, well down the column, gives his own version of the night's doings:

> We had been going for about a couple of hours when my truck halted for about five minutes in a little hamlet – why, I don't know. When it moved on, the yellow bus which we had been following in the column was

nowhere to be seen. My driver stepped on the gas and we shot ahead in pursuit at a good 40 mph. This was too much for the old truck. There was a strong smell of hot bearings and we pulled up. All around were bleak, snow covered mountains and over all a clear glittering expanse of star filled sky. It was bitterly cold, about 1 o'clock in the morning and not another vehicle in sight. The driver examined the back axle and conveyed to me that the truck was temporarily out of action. He spoke no English and had no map. I had no idea where we were, or even where we were supposed to be making for. I found out later that the only order to the Norwegian drivers was to 'follow the vehicle in front.' We were completely lost.

The men were huddled down, packed tight in the bottom of the truck for warmth. One of them volunteered to come with me in search of shelter for we obviously couldn't spend the night in the truck in the freezing temperature.

Within half an hour the whole rear part of the column, three buses and about eight trucks had caught us up and were halted behind the broken down truck. Then seemingly out of nowhere, a car arrived on the scene driving south. Out of it got a British officer – a Lieutenant Colonel of the Royal Armoured Corps (RAC). He told the OC A Coy where he was and gave him a telephone number. He then left as he had come – in a hurry. Who was he? Was he genuine? He need not have been, and why was he travelling south? Towards the enemy.

As luck would have it, they found a large farmhouse within half a mile. This, after the usual formalities, OC A Coy broke into and finally got his men and the Norwegian drivers into the welcome warmth of a vast kitchen.

The OC telephoned the Gausdal number given by the RAC officer but had failed to obtain it and suspicions were aroused. At that moment a knock came at the door. There was immediate silence in the kitchen and every man jumped for his weapon. The door suddenly opened and Jepson, the interpreter walked in. He said that Gausdal, where we were heading for, was occupied by the Germans (this was not in fact correct). OC A Coy then inspected the Norwegian trucks and found that they must soon refuel.

The column moved off again as a fighting unit, 7 Platoon in a lorry leading some 200 yards ahead. All rifles and light machine-guns were ready for action and all troops warned that they might have to get out of the lorries very quickly and into action without any more warning than hostile shots. Having filled up the transport with petrol and oil, the missing rear portion of the column ran into Gausdal just as Major Roberts and the last of the D Coy transport was moving out.

Even this last lap was not without its frustrations. The road between Gausdal and Tretten rises up to almost 2,000 feet above sea level with a very steep fall into the Tretten gorge. The front half of D Coy's convoy arrived at Tretten, without incident at some time after 4 a.m. They had embussed in open trucks, mounting Bren guns on the roofs of the cabs and in the rear, while men with fixed bayonets sat on each side, for we fully thought we should have to run the gauntlet. The rear half of the column was stopped owing to one of the trucks overturning on a bend in the road. No one was injured but it took nearly two hours to get the convoy going again. It then met a convoy of empty lorries going in the opposite direction. There were scenes of complete confusion and chaos in the darkness and the deep snow on the narrow mountain road while we tried to get the convoys past each other. The last of West Force climbed the final ridge as the sun came over it from the eastern side. Then we dropped down again between the pine trees into the gorge. At last we crossed the red girder bridge over the River Laagen and we had arrived in Tretten. By this time the troops had spent more than eight hours in the open trucks.

FIVE

148 BRIGADE WITHDRAWS

Monday afternoon, 22 April – East Force. Foresters

In front of the Balbergkamp (Map 5) C Coy had two platoons up the hill on the left of the road, facing south, and the third astride the road. There was a standing patrol in the wood above the forward position. B Coy was on the right of C by a farm house. Half the mortar platoon, under Lt Vallance, was in position to cover the ground between the road and the frozen lake. The house used as battalion HQ of both battalions was a very small and insignificant one and stood about a mile behind the forward positions. About noon, incendiary bombs were dropped on the British position; this was followed by a 100 mm mortar bombardment. While this engaged attention towards the main road, the Germans also began to work around our left flank.

The German mortar fire on the road area made it impossible to bring up the food which had been prepared by the cooks.

OC C Coy was with his forward platoon when the attack began. 'We opened fire on the enemy seen approaching B Coy's position! Shortly afterwards the forward platoon was also directly attacked, but seemed to hold it off well enough until it practically died away.' In this attack B came under small arms fire and suffered their first casualties, one man being killed and two wounded in 11 Platoon. In C Coy's area, mortaring was fairly heavy but it mostly fell on the rear platoon at the edge of the trees. There was a good deal going on beyond the farm in B Coy's area, which by now was on fire and there was an outbreak of firing above and behind us where the standing patrol was. The smoke from the burning farm caused a good deal of confusion. The Battalion IO now warned HQ of B Coy's position and a message came in about the same time from OC B Coy requesting permission to withdraw. In the absence of the two COs the 2IC, Major Dowson, was now faced with a major decision, but nonetheless, he sent orders to B Coy to withdraw and a runner to C Coy and to Lt Vallance to notify them accordingly. At the same time, he ordered Lt Dolphin at about 2 p.m., to take all personnel (about twenty in all) at Battalion HQ, to try to check an enveloping movement by the enemy on our left flank. At this time, bombs from aircraft and 100 mm mortars were very harassing and made communication within the

Battalion, even by runner, very difficult. Lt Dolphin's recollection of his force was one light machine-gun and ten cooks.

The result of the German outflanking movement at the Balbergkamp was a hasty withdrawal northwards up the road by the British. Rations and other stores were jettisoned so as to make room on the available transport for the troops. The narrow winding road gave ample opportunities for attack from the air. Troops on foot were overtaken and outflanked and the Foresters lost a large part of their two companies, which, it is believed, never received the orders to disengage from the enemy.

Control of 148 Brigade seems now to have reverted to the brigade commander. He decided on withdrawal but the method had to be worked out. The only means of evacuating the battalion, which was in close touch with the enemy, was by lorry and the only ones available were those in charge of the quartermaster. Major Dowson was ordered to proceed at once to obtain these lorries. In due course all the troops that were anywhere near the road were picked up and piled onto the lorries. All stores, ammunition and other baggage were dumped on the roadside to make room for them. 2nd Lt Crane undertook to stay behind and blow up the road at a place prepared by the engineers in order to delay as far as possible the German advance. Crane blew his hole in the road at about 2.45 p.m. He then left with his CO and 2IC northwards. The convoy of lorries was bombed and machine-gunned from the air about a mile south of Oyer.

At about 3 p.m. the CO Col Ford was met by the brigadier and ordered to occupy a position in the rear of the Leicesters a mile north of Oyer. He learned from Brigadier Morgan that there was still no news of Major Roberts and his half of the Sherwood Foresters Battalion west of the lake. At this stage, a mention should be made of the attack on brigade headquarters by enemy ski troops. Fortunately, this outflanking movement never developed in any strength and the Foresters were able to clear up the situation round the inn later in the day and so were able to reopen the road between Oyer and the forward troops; but for some hours the situation was utterly confused.

We must now return to the Balbergkampen.

At 2 p.m. 2nd Lt Campbell of C Coy reported German infantry on the road. The Coy commander, Redmayne, ordered him to move up the hill through the trees to cover the rear of the company position. Whilst up there, 2nd Lt Dolphin and his ten cooks passed Campbell's platoon. Shortly before this, a message reached 2nd Lt Fitzherbert and his HQ Coy men, from the Leicesters' IO Coleman, telling him to withdraw to the road and thence by MT northwards. After seeing the situation on his left flank, Captain Redmayne returned to his platoon on the road but could not find them and was told by a sergeant of the Leicesters that they'd had orders to withdraw. He then went down to the bottom of the cliff to the cottage where Battalion HQ had been, to see what the form was. There was no one there and no sound of action from the right of the road. He therefore started up the hill again to collect the rest of the company. At the top he found Lt Ellis nominal BTO but now involved in fighting with his old company, who said that the remaining platoon, though incomplete, had withdrawn down the track which met the road further back and that he thought there were now only Germans along the edge of the trees where the forward platoon had been.

The two officers followed the track down until they met the main road, up which they walked northwards until they came to the piles of kit thrown off the lorries to make way for the troops. Here, a small crater had been blown in the road and they found a motorcycle amongst the other gear. Ellis was sent away on it while Redmayne remained to make sure that no men had been missed who might be making their way down from the hills to the road. One small party eventually came by and were told to push on and try to catch up with anyone who was preparing a position further north.

Not long afterwards, Redmayne heard the exhaust of a motorcycle and presumed it was Ellis returning. He then realised that the noise was in fact German motorcyclists coming from the south. When they saw him, they hastily fell off their machines on one side of the road. Redmayne went over the edge on the other and was lucky enough to fall about ten feet and to end up in a sort of cave under the wall of the road. The Germans threshed about overhead for a bit and then went on. It was not a very brilliant performance on either side. It was then discovered that OC C Coy was missing.

B Company appear to have received their orders to withdraw from their original position shortly after 2 p.m. They moved west across the railway and then made their way northwards to Faaberg station. With Capt. Branston, there were another four officers and forty-four other ranks. At Faaberg station they tried to contact Battalion HQ on the civil telephone, but were not successful. Then they began to receive attention from the air, being bombed and machine-gunned. They moved off northwards up the line. It was then about 4 p.m.

Sometime later Capt. Branston, with the remainder of B Coy, reached the railway/river bridge at Hunderfossen, which they crossed over to the west bank of the Laagen. 2nd Lt Blackburn of B Coy, with three men of C Coy tried to follow the main party over the bridge but came under small arms fire from the east of the main road and failed to make it. They were later taken prisoner on the river bank. By this time not only OC C Coy but also OC B Coy and most of his men were out of action.

Now the REs requested permission to blow two bridges, the road bridge at Faaberg and the rail bridge at Hunderfossen. It was a question which called for quick thinking. Authority for vital demolitions of this kind rested entirely with the Norwegian command, but there was obviously not more than a minute or two left for action. Col Clarke gave orders to leave the road bridge intact but blow the railway bridge. Capt. Branston and his men had only just made it.

The Norwegian divisional commander described the loss of the Faaberg position as the first serious defeat of the war and noted that it would have catastrophic consequences for the Norwegian detachments. His comment invites the reply that no Norwegian detachment was thrown in for its defence, in spite of repeated requests for help and that they alone could have supplied ski patrols to remedy the situation on our left, where small numbers of enemy ski patrols manoeuvred to such great effect along the heights. The Norwegians claimed that their men were utterly exhausted by the skirmishes which they fought during the long ten days when they stood alone, whereas the British felt that theirs had been given no time to adapt to the bewildering physical conditions of the fight. But these are imponderables between which it is difficult to judge; what is certain is that the Germans seemed to need no rest and made the deep snow and unfamiliar terrain their ally.

The preceding chapters give ample opportunities for the armchair critic.

Norwegian criticism of the British attempt to keep the Germans at bay was somewhat unfair for as their own Col Jensen of the Dragoons pointed out, the conditions that the British found themselves in were very much worse than for the Norwegians, who were not only used to them but were also appropriately dressed for them. Neither was there any mention of the British detachments who had suffered just as much with a journey of 500 miles to get there across a storm-tossed ocean, with little food and inadequate clothing for sub-Arctic conditions and now with insufficient means to defend themselves other than their out-of-date rifles. But the real reason for this state was down to the politicians and generals of the day of both countries, who should have seen from the daily press that both would have to confront Hitler sooner or later.

But to return to Norway, no attempt was made to make a stand at Oyer (Map 6) and the reunited battalions moved north again to make a stand at the hamlet of Tolstad just a mile or two south of the village of Tretten.

PSM Shepphard of the mortar platoon of HQ Coy tells us:

> Here, we were in contact with the enemy and could see right across the valley. The rifle companies A and D went forward with D deployed on our left and A company on the other side of the river Laagen. This was where Capt. Ramsden, C Company commander with experience of the Great War, advanced on a machine-gun nest which had been giving us a great

deal of trouble, quite openly, his men following closely with bayonets fixed as they might well have done in that war, but the Germans were waiting for them, and although the nest was silenced, the platoon was badly shot up and Captain Ramsden was killed on the spot.

Corporal Arthur Thomas of C Coy now takes up the story.

Eventually, we arrived at our destination at about 5.30 p.m. and were led through the woods to some high ground in the area of Oyer (Vardekampen heights) with a very substantial rocky outcrop, for which later that night we were to be very grateful. Here we relieved A company of the Leicesters who seemed to be in a very exhausted condition as they'd had nothing to eat for more than two days and very little sleep.

As we settled in to our position our platoon officer asked the OC where the enemy were and he indicated some buildings in front of us at about 2 o'clock and pointed out that they had some very accurate 100 mm mortars. All we had was a two-inch and our rifles. As we lay in our position all we could hear was the sound of squeaking wheels which to us sounded very much like tanks, but as we had been assured that there were no tanks in the area we then thought it must have been farm vehicles. As it turned out we were right the first time, they were tanks.

Some time before 11 p.m. my attention was drawn to the Sherwood Foresters on our left who were returning. Almost at the stroke of 11 p.m. a single shot rang out then all hell was let loose. There was very heavy mortar fire to the front of our position and continuous tracer fire so close overhead we could have reached up and touched it. Jerry obviously set fixed lines on our position. Prior to the attack, we had heard sounds of revelry coming from the direction of the enemy and we understood they were celebrating Hitler's birthday.

Eventually we withdrew through the trees and reached the side of the road where there were drystone walls on each side, but by this time the enemy had also reached the road and one of their machine-gunners had mounted a gun on top of the wall and was firing along the top. By keeping well into the side of the road it was possible to make progress and this was OK for a time, then suddenly, progress stopped and on making my way to the head of the queue, I discovered the reason for the hold up. There was a long gap in the wall and no one wanted to take a chance and dash across the open ground, bearing in mind that there was a full moon and it was unusually light. As the choice was to stay and be captured or shot, I decided to take a chance and I don't think I have ever run so fast, either before or since, and as I had made it the others followed suit, and I was very pleased that the other members of my section had decided to join me. Of the one or two who decided to stay behind, I never saw them again.

We must have walked for miles and came to a clearing where there was a large barn where we spent the rest of the night. Next morning preparations were to go ahead for the building of a roadblock. I was given the task of reconnoitring the hilly country to our right with a patrol. We soon came upon an isolated farmstead where we were given milk to drink and invited to stay and rest.

We lost all track of time and must have made a very wide sweep, eventually coming down to a very wide lake or river with a large number of holes in the ice due to the bombing. In the distance we saw a plane approaching very low so we made for the tall reeds along the shore. The plane passed low overhead and we were convinced that we had been seen but as it didn't reappear we set about rescuing one or two members of the patrol who had fallen into the water during our dash to the shore. All were extricated successfully and having spotted a building some short distance away, we made for this and stripped off what wet clothes we could and cut off the sleeves from our pullovers to use as socks. As we prepared to leave we saw in the distance what we took to be a column of Norwegian troops but on taking a closer look through some field glasses it turned out to be Germans.

After some time, we moved off and came to a bridge (Oyer) and we were challenged by a British officer collecting stragglers with a bus waiting a short distance away. After reporting to the officer, we were told to board the bus as in another five minutes the bridge was going to be demolished. This was confirmed as we drove away by a brilliant flash followed by a very loud rumble.

C Coy was the old Loughborough company and another eye witness Arthur Witherbed, gives his own account of that afternoon of 22 April.

A few of us were made into a patrol and with RSM Holyland, we went forward to try and extricate and support the forward units in the Lillehammer area after the first contact with the enemy advance guard. Shortly after this, the enemy tanks and mobile units got through and many of us were cut off. Eventually, a number of us, including three officers and several wounded comrades gathered in the mountains to the east of Lillehammer to discuss the next moves. The wounded, including RSM Holyland, were taken to the German Red Cross by an officer, where they became prisoners; the rest of us split up into groups to try to get back to the battalion, or failing that, to the coast. Four of us, Sergeant Harold Farley of Quorn, Charlie Burford, Wilf Cholerton and myself decided to go it alone and the next day set off to try our luck. As it turned out, we were unable to either get back to the battalion or the coast before the final evacuation, so we turned east towards Sweden and after about a month of wandering about in the mountains in the snow and extreme cold, during which time we were helped by several Norwegians in many ways, not the least, fed, we eventually made it to the border where we were interned with about two hundred others representing most of our regiments in our division. Having suffered frostbite during our trek across Norway, my feet were in such a bad state that after I got back home I was medically downgraded which put paid to my hopes of staying in the Leicesters.

Another comrade, H.C. Harris remembers:

As we had no transport of our own because of the torpedoing of the transport ship *Cedarbank*, when we arrived in Tretten we found we had to commandeer some trucks from the Norwegians who were coming back from the front in droves. When we got somewhere in the area of Oyer, we got out of our trucks just as a Jerry aircraft dropped a bomb and machine-gunned us, which caused a lot of confusion amongst the troops who had never experienced this before. Then we were deployed forward and provided overnight protection on the eastern ridge of the valley, to take the first knock. We duly took it and as we were rejoining the battalion on completion of our task and in the first exchanges of gunfire, we lost our company commander Major W.E. Garner. Fighting all the way now, we gradually closed the distance between ourselves and the rest of the battalion, but progress was slow through the trees and the deep snow and very soon it became clear to us that the battalion we were trying to reach had been forced further back, so some of us were cut off, but a few succeeded in rejoining their comrades. This must have been about the end of B Company. 2nd Lieutenant Jessop and his platoon held a roadblock about two miles north of Oyer for about four hours being subjected to heavy and short-range machine-gun fire. In spite of this and heavy casualties the position was held, although the enemy had penetrated on both flanks and this was where we lost contact with the battalion, but Jessop evaded capture and with some of his platoon managed to rejoin the battalion some eight hours later. One or two of my comrades were going to surrender, but about eight of us decided to make a break and try to rejoin the battalion and when darkness fell we went round our dead comrades and took the iron rations out of their battledress trouser pockets and headed for the hills.

My pal, Johnny Turner was shot through the lower part of his abdomen and he was in great pain and it was obvious the wound had become infected, causing his lower abdomen to swell badly. We carried him on a makeshift stretcher for about three days when we met some Norwegians who took him to a German first aid post; he eventually died from his injuries and his name is the last one on the War Memorial at Melton Mowbray.

We broke into many houses in the hills and the mountains, some of which had been deserted by their owners, and this was the only way we could live. We were well and truly lost and it was very difficult walking in the snow during the daytime when it was very deep and soft, but at night it froze solid. My hands were a mass of chillblains and my feet and legs were so cold I couldn't feel them. We were helped by a few Norwegians who gave us directions and fed us and one gave us a letter to hand over when we got to the border. We eventually arrived at the border on my twenty-first birthday and crossed over it near a farm and I gave the farmer the letter. His wife then appeared and indicated with her hands that she was going to give us a drink for we were all very thirsty and ravenous with hunger.

Her husband must have telephoned the police, for the next thing we knew, a big army truck arrived which took us all off to a camp at Falun, near Gothenberg, where we were interned. Eventually, we were exchanged for some German pilots and were sent back to Scotland by way of Iceland.

The position at Oyer came under heavy gunfire and by about 7 p.m. on 22 April, the position was abandoned and another intermediate position was taken up at the hamlet of Tolstad (Map 3). This had a clear field of fire down the road and was held until about noon on 23 April.

The possibilities of making a stand at Tretten, which is the lowest point at which the Gudbrandsdal valley narrows to a gorge, had been in the minds of the Norwegian high command for some days and rudimentary machine-gun posts had been constructed. The west bank of the river Laagen is here a precipice except for a narrow ledge which carries the railway, while the east bank leaves only enough room for the main road. This winds between the river and a mountain saddle some 1,200 feet high, which is crossed by a farm track running parallel with the road. The village itself is about a mile further north, clustering round the bridge by which West Force had just rejoined the rest of 148 Brigade. The defence of this bridge for at least one clear day was deemed essential by the Norwegian commander-in-chief, to enable Norwegian forces under Colonel Dahl to rejoin the main body. For this reason, a stand had now to be made whatever the cost, instead of a fighting withdrawal from point to point up the valley.

It is true to say that the ensuing engagement on 23 April with the Nazis was lost before it had begun, since the British Territorial troops had been without both food and sleep for more than thirty-six hours. They had lost much of their equipment and were without supporting arms. The troops from the west bank of Lake Mjosa, who had just rejoined them, were in scarcely better shape after nearly eleven hours of freezing travel in open trucks.

On the previous day, two fresh companies, B and C of the Leicesters, had also joined the brigade from Aberdeen. What remained of the

1/8 Foresters East Force had been moved back by the CO at midnight in buses to Tretten.

At about 1 a.m. RSM Carter passed a message to the CO to the effect that the Leicesters' position had been overrun (this was, as it turned out, wrong information). At 2 a.m. the CO met Major Atkin of the Leicesters and the two of them made a joint plan for the defence of Tretten. A composite company of Foresters under Captain Renwick, consisting of two platoons under two subalterns respectively, would take the left of the main road facing east. Major Atkin with his Leicesters would cover the position between the road and the river. These positions were taken up.

At 3 a.m. Brigadier Morgan came in and ordered Col Ford to find Lt Col King-Salter and to take up a position as indicated by King-Salter. This position had been partly prepared and the brigade staff were put under OC Foresters for use as fighting troops.

About 4 a.m., the reinforced East Force embussed once more to the new position indicated by King-Salter. This was generally referred to as the Tretten position. It was about three miles south of the village and the vital bridge. Here the eastern wall of the valley closes in like a great thumb, ending in the Vardekampen heights, around 1,800 feet above sea level and with a steep drop down to the river Laagen. The equally steep wall of the western bank formed a gorge through which the icy Laagen flows down to Lake Mjosa (Sketch B).

In the summer a brook runs under the road alongside a farmhouse called Rindheim. In April this is frozen up and covered with snow. Immediately to the north of the brook, and almost under the shadow of the great bluff behind it, is a clearing or field. This field is irregular in shape and perhaps two to three hundred yards long running away from the road and about half that width across (it is indicated on Sketch B). A few deciduous trees stood on the rocky slope between the field and the road and below the road there was an almost sheer drop of a considerable distance down to the river. At one point the road itself is cut out of the cliff. South of the field and the frozen stream, stood unbroken pinewoods nearly as far as Tolstad, some two miles further south. A more unpromising position for a rearguard action would be hard to imagine.

Various times are given by various people for the arrival of West Force at Tretten and it seems clear that they in fact arrived in several instalments between 4 and 5.30 a.m. At Tretten, they found elements of the battalion transport personnel with, most welcome of all sights, several dixies full of stew and hot tea. The weary, dirty, half frozen and cramped occupants of the trucks tumbled out, got stew and tea and were put into reasonable order under cover so as to get some sleep.

The main building in Tretten was and rebuilt, still is, a cheese factory. 8 and 9 Platoons of A Coy slept in the bomb-proof cellars of the big grey stone building, while 7 Platoon dossed down in the store room and did full justice to the milk, cream, butter and cheese that they found there. Just as well too, as the building was in flames later in the day.

Major Roberts ordered D Coy to take up a defensive position on the west side of the river bridge, facing up the Gausdal road down which West Force had come into Tretten that morning. One section from A Coy was ordered to mount its Bren light machine-gun (LMG) at the east end of the bridge, sited to fire down it.

Tretten itself was only a hamlet. On the east side the mountain came down, thickly wooded, steeply onto the road. On the west of the road a bank sloped down to the river and beyond that the railway, all running north and south. As far as the eye could see along the top of the west bank were cars; some of which had been machine-gunned from the air and riddled with bullet holes and run off the road. Others had simply run out of fuel and had been ditched. Beyond the railway, the opposite side of the valley rose steeply upwards. The village appeared to be destitute of inhabitants.

Having got his men fed, protected and now resting, OC A Coy, who had been out to the bridge on a commandeered pushbike, now got down to some breakfast in the cheese factory. While he was eating it, OC D Coy came in, followed by the adjutant of the Leicesters, Capt. Ford-Smith. Ford-Smith was concerned over an uncovered road junction about two miles west of the river and suggested that a company should push out there to prevent the Germans getting round the right flank. The two Foresters Coy commanders agreed that it looked too dangerous to ignore, but also that they could do nothing about it. Major Roberts had gone off into the blue, D Coy was already in a defensive position and A Coy in reserve, awaiting orders.

On arrival at Tretten that morning, OC West Force, Major Roberts, attempted to find Brigade HQ. Part of the Leicesters HQ was located in the village, and their adjutant reported that Brigade HQ was some three miles to the south and was then engaged with the enemy, together with the remnants of the 1/5th Leicesters and East Force, 1/8th Foresters. As the enemy had now crossed the lake north of Lillehammer, it meant that our right flank was now exposed. OC West Force had therefore placed D Coy on the west bank of the river to guard the approaches to the Tretten bridge. A and half of HQ Coy were sent to the creamery to feed themselves and prepare and send out some food to D Coy, and to hold themselves in readiness for further orders.

At about 7 a.m., OC West Force went south with his acting adjutant Lt R.B. Bradley, to get in touch with Brigade HQ. In due course they found Battalion HQ and reported to Lt Col Ford, informing him of events since separation at the port of embarkation (Rosyth) on the night of 16/17 April and included details of the withdrawal of Dahl Force and the employ-ment of West Force throughout as the rearguard, the few casualties suffered and the extremely exhausted state of the officers and men from lack of rest and food. Having thus reported to his commanding officer, OC West Force relinquished his independent command and resumed his appointment as 2IC 1/8 Foresters.

The British expected the main German attack on their eastern flank, where the snow-covered mountain saddle was accessible and where the farm track also outflanked the road. Two companies of the Foresters were therefore set to control the main road on a three-quarter mile frontage, with the one fresh company of the Leicesters high up on their left flank. This flank was further strengthened by the remnants of three squadrons of Norwegian dragoons, with four medium machine-guns and a mortar, which Brigadier Morgan had induced General Ruge to place under his command. They were posted behind the Leicesters on the plateau formed by the saddle. One company of the newly rejoined Foresters was left to guard the railway line on the other bank.

The situation as described by the CO to Major Roberts was not a happy one. The previous day's engagements had reduced the numbers of the original East Force considerably but at least the second half of the Leicesters (B and C Coys) were now on the scene and the timely arrival of West Force, practically intact, was an unexpected reinforcement. Unfortunately, everyone, except the uncommitted C Coy of the Leicesters, was dog-tired.

Col German with his fresh B Coy had, as we have seen, been shelled out of Oyer at about 7 p.m. the previous evening and had been holding all night a position astride the road near Tolstad, some two miles south of the Foresters at Rindheim. OC Foresters had the remnants of East Force and about thirty personnel from Brigade HQ. 2nd Lt Fitzherbert's composite platoon was in the area of the farm buildings and 2nd Lt Dolphin's beyond them, both covering the buildings. A roadblock was ready to be let down at a bend in the road, while the fresh C Coy of Leicesters was up on the left flank on the slopes of the mountain, some 1,000 yards from the road. At 8.30 a.m., B Coy of the Leicesters could be heard heavily engaged with the enemy. They took the first knock as they were rejoining the battalion on completion of their task and in the first exchanges lost their Coy commander, Major W. Garner. Progress was slow through the forest. They were cut off by the enemy and very few of them succeeded in rejoining their units. Later that day C Coy commander Capt. Ramsden was killed.

Major Roberts, on the way back to Battalion HQ after his reconnaissance, met the military attaché, Lt Col King-Salter, who was now attached to Brigade HQ. On being acquainted with the arrival of West Force at Tretten, he asked for one of its companies to be brought up. OC Foresters approved and A Coy was sent for.

OC A Coy takes up the story.

At about 10.15 a.m. I was asleep in the office of the cheese factory and was awakened by the return of Ford-Smith with a lt col and a major who I didn't recognise. I was given orders by this strange colonel to get my coy up to the line right away, two or three miles out of the village, round a big bluff of rock, which he said I couldn't possibly mistake, as far as the second group of houses. There I would meet a Major Jones of the Pay Corps, who would take over two platoons. The third platoon would have to take up a position to cover the road and 'I think you ought to get a move on.'

I asked this officer, who wore the badges of the Rifle Brigade, who he was. He seemed surprised, but then told me I was quite right to be careful. He gave his name as King-Salter and was showing me his papers when Ford-Smith came into the room and confirmed his identity. Ford-Smith was killed in action later in the day.

I got CSM Hunt busy getting A Coy fallen in, with some anxiety, because of constant air attention from the Luftwaffe, and collected the transport, a truck and two buses. We got the men in somehow, uncomfortably crowded, with the company reserve ammunition in the truck. All weapons were loaded. As I got in beside the driver of the truck, in the lead, Major Dowson appeared and wished us luck. I left behind 2nd Lt Sketchley with CQMS Lindley and two men, with orders to prepare a hot meal and send it up to us as soon as possible. Then I took A Coy towards its first action. The time was about 10.30 a.m.

Major Jones was at the rendezvous beyond the bluff, where a cart track led off the road into the forest. Here Sergeant Rouse with 8 Platoon and 2nd Lt Wright with 9 Platoon debussed and filed off behind Jones. OC Company with 2nd Lt Crawford took on 7 Platoon and reported to the CO. The CO said he was pleased to see me and that they'd had heavy casualties. He looked about done in. Battalion HQ was in a rock sangar about 2–300 yards behind the foremost posts. Visibility was poor because of the trees, the road on the right and the extent of the muck field on the left.

OC A Coy then gave orders to send his transport back a little way along the road and set off to check on his company. He had reached the cart track when up came Col German CO, of the Leicesters, who at that time were withdrawing through the Foresters. The time was about 11.30 a.m. He looked pretty whacked and I offered him a drink from my flask. He said it was the first drink he'd had for twenty-four hours. He then set off to find Col Ford, while OC A Coy resumed his way up the snow-covered track in search of his two platoons.

Tuesday, 23 April

Fighting began on the east bank of the river at about 1 p.m. Three tanks began to force their way along the road into our forward positions unchecked by our anti-tank rifles, which failed to penetrate the armour. A battalion account gives the time of the German attack as about 12 noon.

The enemy on the west bank of the river had by now advanced level with our position at Rindheim and could be seen getting machine-guns and heavy mortars into position on the high wooded slopes. The road-block of heavy trees was replaced after the Leicesters had gone through, but there was insufficient time to interlock the timbers satisfactorily before it was attacked by heavy tanks. This was the first indication we had that they had anything heavier than tracked troop-carrying vehicles. The leading tank struck the roadblock at high speed displacing some of the baulks of timber. The impact caused the tank to leave the road, where it narrowly missed slipping down the bank and into the river. Other tanks succeeded in battering a way through the obstacle and pushed through the forward posts along the road.

Simultaneously with the tank attack, the left flank of the position was attacked and C Coy of the Leicesters was forced to give ground.

The enemy next brought into action his 100 mm mortars and machine-guns, which were on the opposite slopes across the river, and subjected our right flank to a heavy bombardment. This fire, together with the fire of five heavy tanks, made untenable the position of the forward and reserve platoons in the neighbourhood and astride the road; consequently, these were forced to withdraw up into the wooded slopes to the east of the road. Here they took up positions facing the road and successfully prevented the enemy infantry from advancing up it. The centre of the position was still holding its ground.

A tank is a formidable animal when you possess nothing to stop it with. The thick pine woods, the rocky and very uneven ground were obviously not tank country, but at least provided an opportunity for us to get out of their way. The forest did not provide cover against mortar fire and there was always the enemy infantry, infiltrating through the trees, to watch for. One tank using the cart track leading off the main road tried to cut off Battalion HQ, but the attempt was seen in time and Col Ford, Major Roberts and Capt. Athorpe managed to cross the track and reach some boulders where the tank was unable to follow.

All available men were now collected in a new position well up on the boulder-strewn base of the mountain, at the rear of the original battle position. From here the road could still be covered and the enemy's infantry was held up until 4 p.m. by which time ammunition had run out and many casualties had occurred.

OC A Coy, far up the cart track in an apparently fruitless search for his two platoons, heard the mortar bombardment down below him in the road area and retraced his steps, together with two men of his company who had been ordered to take spare ammunition to the two platoons and were similarly lost. By the time they reached the muck field, bullets from small arms fire were whipping across it from the far side. 7 Platoon was engaging this target and was firing into the base of the trees across the field. We had precious little cover from fire, although, firing through a gap in the fence, we were hidden from view. At that moment a good deal of firing seemed to come from our right rear towards the road and someone shouted 'look out, they're behind us.' I picked up the Bren, and with the two other LMGs, moved down off the path and into the trees, and not a moment too soon, for a few moments later a tank had come up the cart track and was shooting up all it saw.

In the trees OC A Coy ran into his CSM, J. Hunt. We made our way down to the edge of the wood towards the road when we suddenly saw the turret of a tank. It was stationary and tucked close into our side of the road. Another tank was stationary some thirty yards ahead of the first. The tank was engaged at almost point-blank range with an anti-tank rifle and Brens without success and then withdrew.

At about 2 p.m. the Germans started shelling from behind the wooded slopes of the hill on the west bank with a 150 mm howitzer. The shells screamed over the top of the hill and landed amongst the trees. By about 4.30 p.m. the position at Tretten was being heavily engaged with tanks. It was learned later that one of the centre platoons under Lt Dolphin had held out in a well concealed position until 6 p.m.

At about 2 p.m. OC D Coy, Major Kirkland, was ordered by King-Salter, on Norwegian advice, to move his company to the south along the west bank of the river, i.e. down the railway, to try to enfilade the German advance on the east bank. A guide was to meet D Coy at a given rendezvous and would lead it to the position on the flank, by a farm called Holsteinsveen, but at about the same time enemy tanks were seen on the road between Tretten and the forward troops. Stragglers were now arriving in the village from the 'front', having made their way back along the edge of the forest. It must have been evident at Brigade HQ that the tanks had got the Rindheim position sewn up. This made the supply of food or ammunition to the forward troops impossible.

A counter order reached Kirkland just as the company was about to move off. The new order directed him to leave one platoon west of Tretten bridge and to bring the other two across to the east bank to form a bridgehead facing south. The right flank was held only by Lt Esam, 2nd Lt Kirk and thirty men of 18 Platoon. With them was Capt. Stoker, the medical officer of West Force.

Kirkland went south of the village with the rest of his company. About a mile out of Tretten, they found a German tank stationary in the middle of the road. An LMG section and an anti-tank rifle immediately went into action, but the tank began to advance down the road towards them. As earlier above Rindheim, there was nothing to do but to seek cover and the troops scattered and made for the forest above them.

Remnants of D Coy Foresters attacking enemy tanks at Rindheim.

From the edge of the trees some 250 yards above the road, we could see open snow-slopes for approximately half a mile back to Tretten bridge. There were two tanks and about fifty German infantry deployed on the road below us, engaged with the forward defences of the village. Word then reached 2nd Lt Parry that Maj. Kirkland had been hit. Parry found his Coy commander lying out in the open about 200 yards from the edge of the wood with his knee shattered. He put a field dressing on the wound and as there was no hope of moving him to cover in the deep snow and under fire he left him. Maj. Kirkland was eventually picked up by the Germans and taken to Lillehammer hospital.

The remnants of D Coy tried to work their way round through the woods towards Tretten bridge, which had been prepared for demolition by Sgt Millington of the Leicesters, but by some mishap was never blown. They'd had some further casualties and took their walking wounded with them. As an organised force, they were out of the fight.

Firing to the south on the Vardekampen stopped about 4 p.m. and at about 4.30 p.m. there were two enemy tanks covering the east end of Tretten bridge, three more on the road and anything up to a battalion of German infantry between the forest and Tretten. There still appeared to be some resistance in the north.

To return now to 18 Platoon of D Coy, west of the bridge. At about 4 p.m. Doc Stoker had word that there were several casualties on the west side of the bridge and he went off to attend to them. Soon afterwards the order to withdraw 18 Platoon was received, as the enemy had got through on the left flank. This order was being carried out when a strong enemy platoon was seen advancing towards our position on the flank. They came with submachine-guns using incendiary and tracer bullets. Luckily the fire was high and not very accurate and a number of the enemy were accounted for before the withdrawal was complete with the loss of only two men. A section of men remained to keep the enemy at bay while the rest of the company crossed the bridge in good order on two lorries supplied for the purpose, and reported to the staff captain (Stafford) on the east side of the river about 400 yards north of the bridge. The remainder of the section of D Coy were now cut off and more than likely were killed or taken prisoner.

At this time the remains of D Coy got down in a defensive position facing west and covering the approaches from the west across the river. The remnants of the Foresters and the Leicesters were now all under the command of Lt Col German.

During the afternoon Brig Morgan and Col Jensen appear to have been watching events from Tretten. Jensen was clearly concerned at the way events were going, particularly as more and more stragglers found their way into the village from the south. He told the brigadier that the British troops were retiring four to five hours before the time fixed and if they continued to do so the Norwegian positions would be jeopardised.

To return to Battalion HQ in the Rindheim area, every effort was made by OC A Coy to get away up the mountainside (Vardekampen) with the object of getting behind the reserve position at Tretten which had been heard engaged with enemy tanks since about 2.30 p.m. But all attempts to get over the mountain failed as a sheer cliff was in front of us. The snow was about two feet deep. The only way to avoid being cut off was to get back through the trees onto the road and head north towards Tretten, but by this time tanks blocked our way.

Collecting individuals and small parties of men, which included Lt Dolphin and most of his platoon, we then continued north, avoiding the road and keeping to the trees above it. We eventually got as far as the village but by this time it had fallen to the enemy and there was no alternative but to continue north through the forest.

It was learned later that one of the centre platoons under Lt Dolphin had held out in a well-concealed position until about 6 p.m. They had then attempted to get back round the east side of the mountain, but failed and consequently joined up with Capt. Beckwith's group. Dolphin himself was taken prisoner some twelve days later along with Beckwith, 2nd Lts Fitzherbert and Crawford, two officers of the Leicesters and a number of men of half a dozen units, including some of 15 Brigade, which had been sent to relieve 148 Brigade north of Kvam. Lt Dolphin was subsequently awarded the Military Cross. At about 5.30 p.m., Doc Stoker was dealing with the wounded in his improvised ADS in the cheese factory. At this time the Leicesters were withdrawing through Tretten and such lorries as were available were quickly loaded up with the exhausted troops and headed north at about 7 p.m. closely attended by enemy aircraft with machine-guns and bombs. Shortly afterwards, Stoker left the village which was deserted and was being heavily shelled. He subsequently joined Col German's party and was captured with them five miles north of Ringebu on 27 April.

The true facts came to light later from an officer of the Leicesters in a POW camp in Germany. He and others had headed north up the road from Tretten, hoping to be shuttled back in whatever transport could reach them. One truck arrived down the road and lifted all those it could carry. With it came a senior officer who ordered the remainder of the troops to hold the road where they were; transport would be sent back for them, but it never came back.

This party of troops, including Capt. Lubbock of the Leicesters, Lts Esam and McConnel of the Foresters and a number of men from both units, took up positions on both sides of the roadway. Slowly the daylight faded, but no truck came back for them. At dusk, a German tank rounded the corner from the south. Everyone there knew there was nothing for it but to seek cover and they raced for the trees. A tank rumbled towards them and stopped close by and a voice called out in English 'Come out Englishmen, it is alright.' Jack Esam was the first to get up and go forward. A shot from the tank killed him. Doc McConnel ran forward to Esam and was shot down, then the tank guns opened up in earnest and sprayed the edge of the wood. Very few escaped alive.

This, then, was the situation after the battle of Tretten, after which what was left of 148 Brigade dispersed with the help of transport mustered in the rear, to seek refuge forty-five miles back in the Heidal.

SIX

THE END OF 148 BRIGADE AND 15 BRIGADE DEPLOYS

D o you remember that St. George's day? Do you remember Tretten Gorge? Do you remember the hellish din of warfare on that late sunny afternoon, the confusion, men shouting orders, wounded men screaming in pain, the horrendous shriek of the dive-bombers and the explosion and dust of their bombs and the deadly song of flying shrapnel? The high-flying bombers and the dying whistle of their bombs and the earth shaking crump as they struck the ground all mixed in with the explosions of the mortar and cannon fire, the crack of bullets as they passed too close to your ears; and not forgetting the aircraft as they roared up and down the gorge firing their machine-guns at everything that moved. It was here that the remains of the Leicesters, the Sherwood Foresters and the Norwegians fought shoulder to shoulder. It was an unequal battle which did little more than delay the German advance. We had nothing with which to boost our morale and very little ammunition for our rifles. Yet how did we manage to leave more German dead behind us than our own? If only we'd had more support and some more and better equipment, the battle for Norway might even have had a different ending.

I was awakened shortly after I had fallen asleep it seemed, by the urgent hand of Corporal Dunkley shaking my shoulder.

'Come on Lofty, wake up, we've got to go on patrol and find the colonel. The OC has already gone to see where he is and should have been back ages ago.'

I struggled to get to my feet and legs which had no feeling in them and were stiff with cold, along with the others who made up our patrol. It must have been about 3 a.m. and just beginning to get light on 23 April when we made our way down to Tretten bridge where Lt A.B. Speak was waiting for us. Troops were milling about in a hive of activity in the vicinity of the bridge, with officers and men of the Leicesters, Sherwood Foresters and Norwegians all mixed up together doing their best to strengthen the natural defences of the gorge.

Out of the corner of my eye, while the corporal and the lieutenant were conferring with a Sherwood Forester captain, I saw our Platoon Sergeant

Dick Millington, who was very busy with one or two REs fixing an explosive charge to the bridge. Others were busy constructing road-blocks by felling trees near the gorge and putting them in place on the west side of the bridge on the road from Gausdal. For some reason the bridge was never blown.

It was decided to make up a patrol and send it down the road towards Lillehammer to see what had happened to the CO, Colonel German, and the rest of the battalion.

On the orders of Corporal Dunkley, we got 'fell in' and checked our rifles, making sure there was one 'up the spout' just in case and that the safety catches were released. Lt Speak said:

> Right, Lofty. Get out in front of us by about ten paces and after you have walked another ten, stop and listen and keep your eyes and ears wide open, then repeat that until I tell you to stop. Got it? If you see or hear anything that might be – hostile, stop and put your hand up and dive for cover immediately if you can find any. If you are unlucky enough to get shot, don't worry, we'll look after you. Right? Get set then and away you go – we're right behind you.

We had not gone far into the dusk of a pre-dawn, when I began to feel the hairs on the back of my neck begin to stand up as we made our way down the road slowly and quietly in the eerie grey light which precedes daylight, ten paces at a time. On the right, the river Laagen made its way south at the bottom of a steep and wide bank overgrown with wild shrub-bery which could, for all I knew, be the hiding place for dozens of the enemy.

On the left, the rocky wall of the gorge rose up almost vertically, like a cutting some twelve to fifteen feet high then tapered off. After about half a mile and one or two uneventful halts, some snow fell to the ground with a thud from the branches of a tree up on the left – I nearly died of fright with my hand in the air as a signal to Speak, who came forward to me and asked what was up.

'I thought I heard something move up there,' I said nervously.

'Must have been a branch or something,' he grunted confidently, 'Oh well, keep going lad, we're right behind you,' he said.

I carried on, expecting the sudden appearance of enemy troops in the roadway in front of me.

I stopped again and held up my hand after the usual ten paces, but nothing stirred.

I paced onwards down the road into the unknown. Suddenly I stopped in my tracks. Did something move amongst the trees on the opposite bank of the river or was it my tired imagination? I stared hard at the point again until I couldn't say whether it was something or nothing, and my eyes were tired too; it could be a mirage, I thought, but I dropped to my haunches to make myself a smaller target. Speak was by my side in a flash.

'What is it, lad?' he asked anxiously.

'I don't know, Sir, it looked to me as though someone moved behind one of those conifers on the far side of the river, but I couldn't swear to it, could have been imagination.'

'Oh, well, carry on lad, we're ready for them if you stir them up.'

After we had covered a mile or so of this harassing movement, I came to a bend in the road and this is where I heard the sound of marching feet in the distance. I stopped with my hand in the air and Speak was almost at once beside me. By the time the lieutenant joined me the marching feet appeared round a bend in the road and we could just make out the figures of some half a dozen men approaching. Who they were we had no idea as yet, and I kept my forefinger in readiness along the trigger guard.

'I think it's the Major, Lofty – yes – it's him alright – look – they're waving to us.'

When Major German and his patrol came up to us, he looked completely exhausted and red eyed through lack of sleep. He had a gloomy tale. It appears that they went back to the spot where the colonel was last seen at Tolstad and found it had been overrun by the enemy. 'It's not surprising really,' the Major continued, 'They seem to be everywhere, and we'd better get back to Tretten, for soon these roads will become jammed with troops and vehicles, both friendly and otherwise.'

By the time we got back to Tretten bridge, the Luftwaffe had commenced its daily routine and now the high-level bombers started to appear as well as the Me 109s and the twin-engined Me 110 fighter bombers.

'Better get your men over to that wall, corporal, and see if they can bring some of these bastards down.' Speak hissed angrily.

'Yes, but how the hell can we bring down aircraft with these bloody peashooters, and when we've only got a few rounds each of ammo left, that's what I'd like to know, Sir?' Len protested, but before there was time for the lieutenant to answer a high-flying Heinkel bomber flew overhead and dropped a stick of bombs.

As the bombs fell earthwards the very air around us began to vibrate. The crack of an explosion made the ground beneath our bodies heave and tremble. Then the debris began to fall and shrapnel sang and hissed all around us and we were thankful for our steel helmets, something I never saw any Norwegian soldier wearing during my whole time in Norway.

The bombings were very quickly followed up by the low-flying machine-gunning 109s and the 110s.

Colonel German with his 'fresh' B company had been shelled out of Oyer the previous evening (22 April) with several losses. They had been holding a position all night astride the road near Tolstad, some two miles south of Rindheim (Sketch B).

It was about 8.30 a.m. that B Company of the Leicesters could be heard heavily engaged with the enemy at Tolstad, and in the words of PSM Shepphard:

> We found ourselves not far from Tretten village and we were told by Col German to take up a position in an old barn and try and hold it until 4 p.m. Up until now the exercise had been one of delaying tactics and withdrawal with verey lights going up at nights on either side of the valley. It was obvious to us that the enemy were continually outflanking us, also withdrawals nearly always meant that there would be stragglers, some of whom had been wounded by small arms fire and could not keep up with the main body. These were overtaken by the enemy and made prisoners.
>
> From our position in this barn we could see through various holes in the walls across the valley and also down it. After a while we saw a light tank coming up the road towards us, also a section of German infantry advancing along the road on the other side of the river. They came up the road as far as a roadblock, moving in the cover of dead ground and in single file ahead. Then we saw troops with 150 mm field guns forming up and they started to shell Tretten village. By this time it was early afternoon on 23 April. We engaged them with our Bren guns but before he had fired many rounds our Bren gunner was unfortunately killed because our magazines had been loaded with anti-aircraft rounds which meant that in every five rounds there was one tracer which of course gave our positions away to an enemy sniper. Very soon after this we saw three or four tanks a few hundred yards away and we decided to attack them with our anti-tank rifle. I set it up and fired three or four bullets at one of them but apart from the clang as the bullets struck home, nothing happened and they didn't appear to move. But they machine-gunned and shelled the barn for about half an hour, then one of the tanks came right outside the building and although I fired a shot at almost point-blank range, still nothing happened. By this time the hay in the loft above us was on fire and blazing fiercely, and the anti-tank rifle which I held in my hand was suddenly struck by a bullet, and splinters of wood from the stock went into my hand, and the rifle was knocked from my grasp across the floor of the barn. Then we started moving out and blood was pouring from my hand. We not only discovered that the whole building was well and truly on fire but the Germans were waiting for us to come out. They had surrounded the barn. The next thing I knew was being told by a feldwebel that 'For you, the war is over!' They put a field dressing on my hand and put me on a truck with some other prisoners and sent us on our way to Oslo.

By noon on 23 April, the remnants of 148 Brigade had taken up their final position, the Tretten position.

Somewhere around 2 p.m., a report that Austrian ski troops had been seen amongst the trees on the hill to the east of the village caused a certain amount of anxiety amongst our officers. Col King-Salter, who was the most senior officer at Battalion HQ in Tretten, ordered a standing patrol to be sent up into the woods on our eastern flanks to protect our rear. So our own little band under Corporal Dunkley, reinforced with a few more HQ personnel set off once more through the trees to see what the position was.

As we climbed up through the trees in open order, we heard a distinct thud behind us followed by an explosion on the opposite hillside to the west of the river. We stopped in our tracks and watched while several more shells from the enemy's guns came over the top of the hill with the now familiar 'whoosh' and exploded in the forest on our side of the gorge. We realised that we had no answer to this kind of artillery.

We plodded onwards and upwards through the trees and the snow. We could hear the roar of aircraft engines and rifle fire somewhere further down the valley and machine-gun fire from patrolling 190s which gave some idea of just how close the enemy were to Tretten. Occasionally we would see a Ju 52 transport plane carrying enemy troops to Trondheim. We had not gone very far when we saw a khaki-clad figure approaching on skis. He was a man in his thirties, an officer and had all the appearances of belonging to the French Chasseurs des Alpins. Len Dunkley viewed the intrusion of this individual with the deepest suspicion. The man stopped short on his skis and in a heavy accent which could have been French asked Len to direct him to brigade headquarters. But Len wasn't having any of that and his reply was brief and to the point.

'We have no idea where the HQ is and even if we did we wouldn't be able to direct you for these trees.' There was a sudden clatter as Private Bumpus drew the bolt of his rifle back and sent a round up the breech. The officer gave us a disgusted look and a grunt as he pushed himself off with his ski sticks.

'He's either a Quisling or a German dressed as a Chasseur.' Len growled.

The very fact that the man could have been a fifth columnist was enough to put your nerves on edge.

Fighting on the east bank of the river on front of the Vardekampen began about midday. Three tanks began to force their way along the road into the forward positions, unchecked by the anti-tank rifles fired against them. On the opposite bank of the river, the Germans had advanced almost level with our position at Rindheim and could be seen quite clearly getting machine-guns and heavy mortars into position on the high wooded slopes. The roadblock of heavy trees was replaced after the

Leicesters had passed through at about 11 a.m., but there had been insufficient time to interlock the timbers satisfactorily before they were attacked by heavy enemy tanks.

Simultaneously with the tank attack, the left flank of the position was attacked and C Company of the Leicesters were forced to give ground. Arthur Thomas of C Company remembers seeing Private Bob Holt calmly cleaning his rifle after their initial brush with the Germans and was impressed by Bob's unruffled attitude.

All the while, stragglers of both battalions were coming in from the burning woods on the east of the river, most of them without ammunition. By this time our little band were now down to one round each and Len Dunkley ordered us to keep this in our rifles for emergency. One or two of our badly injured comrades were being carried on stretchers to the First Aid Post in the cheese factory. An officer who had been shell-shocked in the First World War was seen trying to stop an armoured car approaching the bridge with his revolver and was removed from danger just in time. In the words of Norman Barnett of the Leicesters HQ signals platoon 'By mid-afternoon small arms ammunition was beginning to run out and most of the Brigade had not eaten anything for almost a week and had not been able to rest. All this time Tretten was being bombed and machine gunned from the air.'

At about 4–4.30 p.m. Col German of the Leicesters took over an anti-tank rifle from Corporal Mee and fired several rounds at one of the tanks approaching the bridge. With a very lucky shot he managed to hit one of its tracks in a vital spot and put it out of action. This was indeed a lucky shot for the half-inch bullets wouldn't pierce armour. What we needed very badly was artillery, mortars and aircraft and last but not least proper clothing for operations so close to the Arctic Circle.

At about 6 p.m. the Leicesters started withdrawing through Tretten and most of us of Battalion HQ boarded one or two lorries which were available and made off down the road towards Ringebu. Considerable loss was suffered at Tretten and out of nearly 2,000 men the Foresters and Leicesters were now reduced to 300 men and nine officers between them. The Norwegian Dragoons, whose position on the saddle of the Vardekampen heights had not been seriously attacked, were able to get back to their transport along the farm track just before the final abandonment of Tretten. A small number of Leicesters made their way through by the same route over the saddle and into the village, where they were able to pick up a few vehicles which were being used to carry the most exhausted and wounded men away from the battle area. Other stragglers continued on foot until they reached the sheltered valley of the Heidal where they were dispersed amongst the houses there.

Our own unit were taken on to Ringebu, a village some 40 miles to the north of Tretten. I found myself sitting on the tailboard and as the lorry went over a deeper pothole I was thrown in the air and landed on my backside on the road watching the lorry disappear in the distance. But the driver stopped and backed up to me. Several times we were attacked on the way by Me 109s. Fortunately we suffered no severe loss and arrived at our destination safely.

On arrival at Ringebu, we were offloaded and our transport returned towards Tretten to pick up any stragglers. Here was what appeared to be Norwegian/British HQ.

But confusion still reigned here, for it was known that the Germans had pushed on immediately from Tretten with an armoured column, and it was also unfortunate that at this time the road to the north between Ringebu and Otta had been temporarily blocked by enemy bombing.

On the river side of the road cars had been dumped and abandoned and Len Dunkley and a few comrades were searching amongst them to find a 'runner'. On the other side of the road I had spotted a likely-looking car parked just off the road and facing the big house. I moved up to the driver's door and saw it was locked, so I withdrew my bayonet, intent on forcing it when I heard a voice addressing me from the other side of the car. I looked up, and down the barrel of a revolver pointed at my chest.

'This car belongs to me, soldier, and you cannot have it. If you want transport there are plenty of cars along the road where you might find one in good order.'

I looked up above the revolver into the face of a Norwegian officer.

'I'm sorry, Sir, I thought this one had been abandoned.'

On this same Tuesday evening, 23 April, the greater part of the 15th Infantry Brigade under General Paget had landed at Aandalsnes comprising the 1st KOYLI and the Hallamshires; the Green Howards were to follow later.

After the collapse of fighting at Tretten several groups of Leicesters and Foresters tried to make it on foot through the trees, some made it to Ringebu and some were captured, and some even made it to Sweden across the mountains, but not without help from the Norwegians, who fed them and guided them. One party of Leicesters, which included the CO Colonel German, managed to reach Ringebu and later on Venabygd, and marched through the village. There were plenty of soldiers about who ignored them but when they got halfway through, one of the party muttered 'It's the Jerries!'

They marched on, but their luck was about to change for, having successfully run the gauntlet through the village, they were challenged by an outpost sentry on the outskirts and taken prisoner.

Lt Col King-Salter, who was with Col German's party, somehow got separated and was the main character in the drama that happened by the church and at Forrestadstugayordet that Ingvald Enger saw and describes. King-Salter was not with the prisoners lined up on the road. He came up the road from the south with a signals officer. As they came past the church, they saw the others lined up in the road and were challenged. They realised the situation and ran back to seek shelter in the farm they had just passed. King-Salter then said:

> I ran through the farmyard to the further corner behind the building and a muck heap and stopped to get my breath. Moments later I saw a German soldier come past the same building only about five metres away from me. He went round the corner without seeing me and I could easily have shot him, but quickly realised that I would give myself away, but the German went back and disappeared from view.
>
> The situation was desperate and I should have waited but I thought my only chance was to run across some open ground between the farm building and the forest and find shelter there. I did this but the German saw me and quickly opened fire. I was hit by several bullets and fell badly injured. I threw my rifle down as a sign of surrender.
>
> Something made me look down and I saw that my right foot was turned the wrong way round. It was a bad moment for me when I realised I had been taken prisoner so early in the war and badly injured at that. Four German soldiers came to me very quickly and were very concerned with my injuries. They asked for my first aid pack but I didn't have one so they got one of their own and dealt with my injuries as best they could. They made a makeshift stretcher with their rifles and a greatcoat and carried me down to the farm and put me in the farmer's bed.

Later the following day, King-Salter was taken to a field hospital where his right foot was amputated. He remained a German prisoner until he was freed in 1945. After the war, he studied theology and became a priest.

During the confusion at Ringebu, about thirty of us were put into a lorry with a civilian driver, a mixed lot of Foresters and Leicesters and set off up the road towards Otta. We didn't seem to go very far when our driver pulled off the main road and drove up a steep track on the right-hand side. We climbed up this steep track through the forest for about twenty minutes or so and came out onto open undulating countryside beyond the tree line and travelled northwest again.

For about two hours we travelled onwards, up and down and weaving in and out through patches of woodland but always heading north-west along a narrow road. We saw no other traffic and no other human beings for the rest of the journey; occasionally we would catch glimpses of farms tucked away in the valleys but otherwise nothing. It was late and almost dark when our driver pulled in to one of these farms. He got out of his cab and told us in fairly good English:

This is where I was told to bring you, my friends, so that you can rest up for a few hours in the hayloft there. The farmer knows you are to stay for a short while and has prepared it for you, so have a good rest and I will return for you in the morning.

Late the following morning, 24 April, when the sun was well up, we saw a girl come from the direction of the farmhouse with a wooden yoke across her shoulders, from which were suspended two wooden buckets.

I rubbed my tired eyes, unsure of what I was seeing, and watched as she picked her way daintily over the grass between the farm and the hayloft and climbed easily up a small meadow between the buildings on her way to milk the cows.

After almost an hour, the girl finished milking the cows and carried the buckets which were almost full of milk, back to the farmhouse.

Shortly afterwards she appeared with a bucket of milk and some glasses and offered each of us a glass of milk.

As the morning wore on and no truck appeared to pick us up we heard the sound of aircraft engines and the dull thud of bombs exploding not very far away from us. Corporal Dunkley, who was the senior NCO with us, was not very happy with this state of affairs and swore that some nasty Quisling was at work against us. He called for two volunteers to go and find Brigade HQ, which was thought to be at Dombaas, and send some transport to pick us up before the enemy found us first. We were still weak from lack of food and tired from lack of rest.

Corporal Arthur Thomas remembers:

> I do recall that after we left Tretten on the 23rd, we were driven north and billeted in a large house at a place called Sjoa. We were still at Sjoa on the morning of 25 April when we entrained at Otta for Dombaas. The town had been heavily bombed. We were billeted in a house on the outskirts where we quickly found it was impossible to step outside without an enemy aircraft appearing. Volunteers were a bit difficult to find when it came to fetching some tea from nearer the centre of Dombaas. People were beginning to get a bit fed up with being regularly shot at.
>
> During the couple of hours or so when enemy planes were not flying, all available hands were engaged at the station unloading supplies for 15 Brigade who were now in action against the enemy at Kvam.
>
> I remember Dombaas Hotel and the parachutes which were draped over some of the stores at the rear.

Our own little group of Leicesters and Foresters, which had been taken from Ringebu in a lorry and left in a hayloft on a farm to rest up somewhere in the hills to the east of Dombaas, eventually got away by the late afternoon of 25 April after an anxious time waiting for the transport to get us back to Brigade HQ, which had already moved back to the town. A lorry suddenly appeared outside the hayloft and we loaded up quickly. The driver headed back along the road which we had come almost two days ago which prompted a remark from the corporal. 'If we keep going much further along this bloody road, we'll be back in Ringebu with the Jerries waiting to welcome us.'

But there was no need to have worried, for after a short distance, we branched off to the right and to the north-west. Occasionally, we saw transport aircraft in the distance flying troops to Trondheim from Fornebu airport at Oslo.

By the time we got to Dombaas where our Brigade HQ was, the time was about 6 p.m. A train had already pulled in from the coast. A few of its occupants, a battalion of the Green Howards, put their heads out of a window and shouted down to us.

'Where's these Jerries, mate?', one shouted with a laugh.

'You'll bloody soon find out where they are, pal,' Len Dunkley replied gruffly, 'They're only a mile or so down the road there.'

Fortunately, things were fairly quiet.

One of the only buildings of any size which appeared to have escaped the attention of the Luftwaffe was the huge Dombaas Hotel. Here we joined up with the remnants of the Leicesters and renewed our acquaintance with Sergeant Po Chambers.

The following morning, 26 April, all hell broke loose as waves of enemy bombers attacked the town from about 7 a.m. until 6 p.m. We got very little rest and the noise and din going on was almost unbearable. Some of my comrades thought they might have been better off outside in the woods instead of being cooped up in a room in one of the biggest hotels in Dombaas.

Corporal Doug Murfet of D Company remembered the hotel at Dombaas:

> I remember the hotel well, especially the cellar, part of which was blocked off. It had a grilled door and behind it was a load of German equipment which convinced me that not all Norwegians wanted the British there. I managed to get hold of a compass which I eventually gave to my nephew when we got back home

While we were resting up in the hotel, we expected to be called out at any moment in support of 15 Brigade. 15 Brigade, except for the five 25 mm Hotchkiss anti-tank guns and the three in reserve, had no better equipment than 148 Brigade, but at least they were able to stop tanks. 15 Brigade comprised the 1st Battalion KOYLI with an extra company made up from the Yorks and Lancs regiment. The 1st Battalion of the Green Howards were in reserve.

Of these troops, only the KOYLI and the brigade anti-tank company plus some REs had reached the position at Kvam by the morning of 25 April.

In the middle of the River Laagen there is a flat pear-shaped island easily accessible from the road over ice and shallow water, but separated from the far side by a deep and swiftly running channel.

Brigadier Smythe placed his HQ at the centre of the village, some distance in front of the church, and disposed his forward companies to cover the road, one from the front edge of the island, where bushes and shrubs give some cover, the other company on the hillside to the north. There they awaited the enemy forces which had already disposed of 148 Brigade.

Private Sydney Barthorpe of the Sherwood Foresters now tells of his experiences:

> It was rumoured that the British were to evacuate within 36 hours. Sgts Rouse and Davies, Cpls Kirk and Houlton and I were separated from our

Private Sydney Barthorpe of the Sherwood Foresters.

company at Tretten and trying to get to Aandalsnes when we met three Norwegian officers who were trying to catch up with their own regiment, heading the same way on the road to Otta. It appeared that the Germans had broadcast a message saying the Norwegian troops could lay down their arms and go home if they wished. This is what these officers were doing. Their names were Captain Ole Bergseth, Lt Rypdal and 2nd Lt Hofseth.

We left Punjen Seter about midnight, making our way north, walking easily on the deeply frozen snow crust. Every now and then one of the lieutenants would go scouting ahead on skis to see if any patrols were about. If any were spotted we made detours but were still able to stick to the right direction. We spent the time walking and trying to get to know one another. In the early stages we got the impression that they thought the British had let them down, but we got on very well together.

At the end of this day we came to a large ski hostel named Peer Gynt. Here we found some venison tubs in the attic. There was no shortage of logs outside, so we were able to keep quite warm.

When we left, there didn't seem to be any danger so we travelled in daylight, but were often going knee deep in snow. That night we stayed at a place near Vardhoj. On the next day we saw Fieseler Storch spotter planes patrolling the area. We arrived at Haugesietri and took a short rest before carrying on to Breidjoriet, where we spent the night.

On the following morning, the two lieutenants were scouting around and it was quite some time before they returned. When they did return, the three Norwegian officers got together and had a serious discussion. We knew by the looks on their faces that all was not well. They came to us and said the situation was serious. We were surrounded by Germans and today they would have to say goodbye, for if they stayed and were caught with us, they would certainly have been shot for helping us to escape. We exchanged souvenirs and addresses, and set off once more. The Norwegians stayed with us for about one mile, then we stopped and shook hands, but before they left they said; 'If any of you could have spoken Norwegian, we could have taken you as one of us.' It was with sorrow that we waved them goodbye.

From now on we had to go back to doing our own thinking. Our position at this time was in the high Rondane mountain area around Dovre. The whole area was like a snow desert. We walked and walked with no food and nowhere to sleep for two days, then at 3 a.m. on the third morning, we saw the dim outline of three bungalows. Had we known they were in a dangerous position, I think we would have passed them by, but in our condition they were a welcome sight. We searched each building for food and then settled down in the one with most bedding. After cooking ourselves a meal we got down to some well needed sleep.

We awoke at 11 a.m. the following morning and got a real shock. The

Germans were only about two hundred yards away filling up shell holes in the road. This was a very unhealthy situation. Behind us was just bare snow-covered mountain with no cover whatsoever. There was a forest about half a mile beyond the Germans, but our only hope of getting there was if the Germans decided to go to their field kitchen for a meal, leaving the road clear for us.

We sat wondering what was to be our next move, when for some reason someone suggested that if we were going to be another three days without food we had better eat, while the enemy dispersed. Like fools we lit the fire to cook something, none of us thinking about the smoke. Sergeant Davies went out with the binoculars to keep a lookout in case they came across to our bungalow to see whether anyone was in hiding. Unknown to us, they were curious about the smoke, but instead of coming frontalwise, the Austrian mountain troops did a wide detour and came up behind us without being seen. One officer went up to Sergeant Davies, who was still looking through the glasses and tapped him on the shoulder.

'Don't bother about them,' he said, 'the war is over for you.'

Four of us were sat round the fire. I was stirring the coffee and Bert Rouse was seeing to some pearl barley. The door was in the far corner behind us; we heard nothing until a voice said, 'Come on, get dressed.'

I stood up and looked round and found myself looking down the barrel of a Luger. In all, five officers stood behind us, three of whom could speak English. They asked us to get dressed once more, then took us out onto the road.

Then the questions came.

'What regiment are you. What ship did you come on, What day did you land?'

We gave them no answers. They demanded again an answer to these questions, saying;

'If you don't tell us we'll shoot you.'

We didn't give much for our chances anyway, however, at that moment a staff car pulled up and out jumped an Austrian Alpine major. He came over to the lieutenant in front of us and it was soon obvious that they were falling out. Not knowing any German we could not follow the conversation. The major drew his pistol on the lieutenant then called some of the troops and we were marched away.

These men were friendly and did their best to try and converse with us. Eventually we ended our journey at Dombaas Tourist Hotel. We were kept in the ballroom which was below ground level and were fairly well treated. Our time was spent cleaning the dining hall and loading lorries with captured materials. During the few days we were there, the major asked us where we had come from and we said Tretten. He asked us how and we told him on foot the whole way, which seemed to surprise him and he also said:

112

Dombaas Tourist Hotel.

'You British fought well at Tretten, I was there too.'

I had some Norwegian kroner and asked him if I could go to their canteen and buy some chocolate and he said 'With pleasure'. So I went round to the canteen window and was met by the lieutenant who had captured us and he said, 'Chocolate? Not for you, English swine.'

I went back and told the major and he said, 'Give me the money and you can have mine.'

A few more prisoners were brought to us, so they said they were sending us to Germany. We set off on open lorries and finished the journey by bus, some of the scenery especially round Tretten was familiar to us.

On arrival at Oslo we were put in the prison which was quite close to the dockyard. Twice a day they took us for exercise in a small orchard. We could see the ships loading and unloading. On our first day here, they tried to get information from us by coming round with sheets of foolscap paper, saying:

'You can write home telling them what you wish, your letters will not be censored. If you play football you can ask for footballs. If you wish, you can tell them when you came to Norway and what ships you came in.'

We did not fall for any of that rubbish so they tried another approach. One at a time, they took us into another room, where a young interpreter started to soft-soap us. He asked me about my parents, brothers and sisters, then he told me about his family, then he suddenly said:

'What ship did you say you came on?'

'I didn't say,' I replied.

Then he said what a wonderful time we would have in Germany. Then came more questions, trying to catch me off guard.

When they found they were getting nowhere, the attitude changed and I got the boot through the other door. I was then taken to another room so that I could not tell the others what was going on.

But before I proceed any further with my story and now that I am a prisoner of war, I must say that from being very young I was having premonitions of experiences that were actually going to happen to me during the war and I used to wonder if any other people had similar experiences, but I never got to know. It was when I was about nine years old we used to have 'silent reading' at school while the teacher marked our books. For some unknown reason, I took out my geography book. Looking through the pages I came to a story and the heading was 'Poland – the Land of the Rainbow'. It was some little time before I could take my eyes off the title – it seemed to have a message for me. I read about the bears in Galicia, the wolves and the wild boar and bison that roamed the forests of the Carpathian Mountains. Nothing more happened until I was about eleven years of age and was going to school one day when I heard the word, Posen, quite clearly as though it had been spoken. I was to hear this word on many occasions but it didn't mean a thing to me. I got a bit nearer to the message when we bought a Ferranti wireless set about a year later. Looking at the stations I saw Posen Military and Posen Civil and for the first time realised it must be a large town, but where did it all fit in? Every time I passed the set I was drawn to the word Posen and wondered what it was trying to tell me. Another day, I had been playing with my friends and sat on a log daydreaming when I quite clearly saw three Viking longboats going past and there were high mountains on either side, and the water was quite calm. I saw myself in one of the boats and this confused me more than ever. But nothing happened until I was called up. I was in the Sherwood Foresters TA and we were billeted in a chapel, in Barnbygate, Newark. It was 3 September and we were sat on the pavement by our billets. People had their doors open so we could hear the 11 o'clock news to see if war was going to be declared against Germany. I heard on the radio that the Germans were fighting the Poles near Posen. I said, 'That's it, lads, we are going to Poland.' But events didn't turn out as I'd thought and eventually we went to Norway. Here, my premonition of the Viking longboats came true. There were no longboats but three cruisers instead and I was definitely in one of them, HMS *Galatea* in fact, and there were huge mountains on either side of us and we were sailing up the Romsdal Fjord where the surface was like glass. It was a beautiful moonlit night and as I watched the mountains pass by I realised that this part of my premonition had come true, but where did Posen fit in? I was very soon to find out in the weeks ahead.

After about a week in Oslo, we were taken down to the quayside and put aboard a collier going to Germany. The ship was MS *Utlandshorn*, which had taken troops from Germany to Norway. It appeared to have had a bit of luck at some time, for a shell had gone through the deck and come out just above the waterline without exploding. The captain of the ship liked to have us prisoners on deck, he said he had seen a submarine periscope and we believed that he thought us being seen on deck might be his passport to safety.

We moored just off Copenhagen for one night continuing on our way early in the morning. In the early afternoon we arrived at the Kiel canal and were surprised at the numbers of barrage balloons which we saw along its banks, especially after reading in the British papers that the Germans thought that balloons were ineffective. We were surprised also at the size of this waterway. It was far wider than we had thought.

We arrived in the port of Hamburg at about 4 p.m. but had to stay on board the vessel. We were allowed to speak to people walking along the quayside and they were just as eager to try their English out on us. To our surprise they seemed quite friendly and no animosity was shown. But things were not to stay the same for very long. That night, about 11 p.m. the RAF bombed the city. Amazingly, they allowed us to walk the decks throughout the attack. The ack-ack guns around the harbour were a rare sight, firing their coloured tracer into the sky. We saw a warship get hit two or three times, warehouses around us also fell to the bombing. Our ship was lifted up by the swell from bombs landing close by. I was not afraid this night, I was really enjoying seeing them getting some of their own medicine for a change.

The morning after the raid, we were not welcome in Hamburg any more. The people who had enjoyed talking to us the day before were now throwing stones and spitting at us. Before being moved some extra men were brought in from a local camp. It was not that they were afraid of us escaping, but more to protect us from the local inhabitants. We were then taken down to the station and put aboard a train. The curtains of the coaches were drawn across the windows and we were warned not to look out until the train was clear of Hamburg. They did not want us to get any pleasure from seeing their damaged city.

After some time on the train we arrived in Berlin. German soldiers offered us thirty Reichmarks for our leather jerkins and blankets some of us had carried from Norway. I did not sell mine but later on wished I had. We were made to get off the train and were marched around Berlin accompanied by loudspeaker vans blaring out to all and sundry that we were Chamberlain's aggressors. After about two hours of marching we were taken back to the train.

The train left Berlin and at about 3 p.m. and the next stop, I could not believe my eyes; when I looked out, the name of the station seemed to hit me between the eyes like a sledgehammer; it was POSEN, and this is where another early premonition came true. So this was where I was to spend the rest of the war – in Poland, Land of the Rainbow. From then on until the end of the war my life was that of a prisoner, but that is another story.

The following is an account of his experiences written by Captain Roger Barratt in his diary while interned at Mora in Sweden:

St Magnus came alongside the little wooden pier at Aandalsnes just in time to be seen by an enemy reconnaissance plane. Disembarkation was carried out as rapidly as possible in case the aircraft above was a bomber and the companies were loaded onto a waiting train. One of the destroyers fired her guns at the aircraft, which very quickly disappeared.

Major Garner and myself joined Major Atkins at a hotel where the Royal Marines had made their headquarters. The marine colonel informed us of the latest situation and all events as he knew them, since the landing of the first part of 148 Brigade during the night of 19 April. It would appear that the original intention had been for the force to proceed to Dombaas, some 60 miles away; organise a base there and then proceed northwards to Trondheim and join issue with the German forces there. But now, reports had been received that a company of German paratroops was causing trouble just south of the town. The colonel then informed us that Brigadier H de R Morgan, the force commander, had decided to deal with these before anything else. Later and from another source, I heard that the brigadier had met General Ruge the Norwegian Commander-in-Chief, probably at Oyer, and had constrained on him to send his force south to assist and relieve the exhausted Norwegian troops somewhere in the region just north of Hamar, just over 100 miles south of Dombaas. These Norwegian forces had met the full force of the German invasion from the start. The colonel was able to inform us that the German parachutists had been overcome and Brigadier Morgan and his force had gone south.

Communication between the base at Aandalsnes and the forward force was almost non existent and had in fact been cut off since early that morning but by about 9 a.m., telephonic communication was again restored and Major Atkins received his orders to bring the fighting part of his force south to Otta, at which place further instructions would be received. By this time the two companies of the Leicesters and the other part of HQ Coy together with stores from the two coasters, departed about 9.45 a.m. for Otta. Personnel of all other sub-units were to remain at the base.

Monday 22 April
The train from Aandalsnes arrived at Otta about 11 a.m. Troops were detrained and AA mountings set up. Some of 148 Brigade personnel were stationed here. Soon after our arrival at Otta, a message was received that we were to proceed further south to a place called Tretten some 45 miles away. B Coy personnel were left at Otta, while the remainder of the Leicesters only, proceeded south by train. These last 45 miles were covered in just over an hour but not without harassment from roving fighters which machine-gunned anything that moved on the road or railway. The train didn't stop but carried on regardless. These attacks were very frustrating for we couldn't hit back.

Eventually, the train pulled into Tretten about 13.45 p.m. to the sound of an air raid siren. This caused a hurried detrainment and dispersal among the trees and huge boulders at the side of the track. In a few minutes a huge aircraft appeared above the station flying low. Someone shouted, 'Don't fire at it for it will give our positions away.'

But the train standing in the station had already given our position away. The plane circled Tretten station twice and disappeared back down the gorge the way he had come.

A Norwegian captain then arrived from Norwegian Headquarters who informed Colonel German and the adjutant that we now came under Norwegian Command. His only orders to us were that we should remain dispersed for protection against enemy aircraft until night-time, when we would receive orders to go forward into the line.

There were six or seven men from A Coy of the Leicesters who had landed in Norway some three days previously. They told a strange tale of an action with the Germans and how they had got lost in the dense forest of conifers and separated from the rest of their company and had eventually found their way back to Tretten.

Not long afterwards, Brigadier Morgan arrived, and it was confirmed that the British force was functioning under the Norwegian High Command, but that any orders received from them were to be confirmed from 148 Brigade HQ before being acted upon. The brigadier gave orders that we were to take up a defensive position on each side of the River Laagen with a weather eye on the right bank, where it was possible

117

that some enemy tanks or armoured cars might be encountered having circumvented the British troops in front.

There were then two possibilities; either the British forces would withdraw through these positions and leave them as the outposts of a new position – or B and C Coys would move forward to strengthen the present positions being held by the Sherwood Foresters and A and D coys of the Leicesters. Accordingly, B Coy took up a position (See Sketch B) to the east of the Laagen, astride a road leading south from Tretten while C Coy took up a position on the Vardekampen heights on the east bank of the river. Fighting personnel of HQ Coy consisted of parts of the MT platoon and the Bren-carrier Platoon under the command of Lt A.B. Speak in the old cheese factory at Tretten.

Several Norwegian troops in lorries were seen about this time retiring through Tretten and within a few minutes the sound of aircraft engines was heard approaching the gorge. The Norwegian soldiers fled from the truck and took to the trees while the inexperienced British troops were hypnotised by the sight of three German fighters roaring towards them up the gorge, all guns firing. In seconds, not a soldier was to be seen; they had flattened themselves on the ground as the bullets pinged off the rocks. In a few moments it was over and the aircraft thundered on up the gorge.

Brigadier Morgan arrived again and gave orders that C Coy of the Leicesters was to proceed forward in buses to a position just north of Oyer. These buses were then to return and transport B Coy to another position at Tolstadt some six miles south of Tretten. (See Sketch B.)

B Coy was then to take up a position some distance to the east of the road right up in the hills. Twice before the British position astride the road had been held, but the Germans had worked round the left flank along the sides of the hills: a thing the Norwegian High Command had said was not feasible. Hence B Coy was being despatched to this position in the hills to prevent a reoccurrence of these German tactics when held up in the valley.

C Coy got away about an hour later, by which time the retirement of the Norwegian forces was in full swing and caused some considerable congestion on the narrow roads. It was considerably more difficult to get B Coy away as the transport never returned. Lorries were commandeered and eventually the first of these got away. Both B and C Coys went forward on the east side of the river and it was now that planes continually swooped to machine-gun the retiring Norwegians along the road. As there was considerable congestion in the Tretten area, it was not surprising that the Germans concentrated their fire power in this area.

Rather foolishly, Bren-gun fire was opened on the offending planes, which of course gave the position away. It was very fortunate that both sides of the road were heavily wooded, which meant that it was fairly easy to obtain visible protection and often protection from fire. At last, all B Coy were collected together and sufficient transport to take them, but every time there was heard the drone of an aircraft engine, the Norwegian drivers would disappear and would not emerge for at least a quarter of an hour. The last of B Coy was taken forward in transport some three-quarters of an hour after the first lot had departed. Meanwhile, the endless stream of retiring Norwegian lorries full of troops continued, making progress against oncoming traffic very difficult.

By this time, the remainder of HQ Coy of the Leicesters had crossed Tretten bridge onto the east side of the River Laagen. Food and ammunition from the train which still remained in Tretten were also brought across the river and dumped in the cheese factory. An HQ was opened in a quarry about a hundred yards forward from the bridge. Round this area small defensive posts were placed. These posts consisted of men from the intelligence section and the signal platoon with one or two from the MT and Bren-carrier Platoons. No orders were received at all as to what this remaining part of HQ Coy of the Leicesters were supposed to do and whether we were to remain an isolated and detached sub-unit. B and C Coys had now been sent forward without any means of communication with Tretten. By mid afternoon a few British stragglers began to arrive back having got lifts on lorries with the Norwegians. They were taken to the first-aid posts in the cheese factory.

It appeared that these stragglers had got lost in the trees in various actions with the enemy, who were expert in setting the trees on fire with incendiary bombs, causing as much confusion as possible, and when they saw the Norwegians retiring they thought a general retirement was taking place and joined with them. Gradually, more and more started to arrive and at about 5 p.m. or soon after, a large party of C Company (40 to 50) men arrived back in considerable disorder under the leadership of the CSM. They told of chaotic encounters with the enemy and swore that many were dressed up in Norwegian uniforms and fired their weapons at them regardless. Then there were the rumours that the Germans were behind them, causing more confusion and panic amongst the troops making them withdraw needlessly. They said that the whole British force was in retreat some miles further forward and that the CO Col German was coming back with them.

It was at about this time that two German Stukas appeared over the gorge and dived on the train in the station. The bombs left the engine intact but derailed one of the carriages. About 300–400 yards north of Tretten bridge, on the east side of the river, there was a large hotel in front of which was an open space. Here, a reorganisation centre was set up, where various stragglers could be organised into their original and proper companies. Some hot tea and rum was also prepared here.

A culvert over a stream some 150 yards south of Tretten bridge and just forward of the quarry caused the road to narrow and a roadblock was prepared. It could not of course be closed until all British troops had retired through that point. Bren guns and those useless anti-tank rifles were put out, covering the approach of all traffic coming up the road. The defensive posts round the quarry were withdrawn now that it was becoming dark, as they were too widely separated to be able to function at all.

At about midnight, over 100 Forester personnel with their commanding officer, Col Ford, arrived in buses having, it was said, received orders to retire. By this time only B Coy of the Leicesters was forward intact, personnel of all other sub-units having retired to Tretten.

Tuesday 23 April

Monday passed into Tuesday unnoticed. About 1 a.m., Major Jones [attached to 148 Brigade HQ] came forward to Tretten by car, with orders from the brigade commander that the forward position was to be held at all costs. It thus became clear that Col Guy German must be informed of this at once and of the present whereabouts of all the troops, as there was no sign of him coming back yet. Major John German was back in Tretten at this time. He knew where the CO had last been at Battalion HQ and so, with persuasion, Major Jones loaned his car for the purpose of taking me forward with Major German to find the colonel.

We drove about four or five miles and then stopped for fear of running straight into the enemy. Jones remained with the driver of the car, while German and I worked our way forward on the road for twenty minutes or so and came to some large buildings and a garage where the colonel had last been seen. It was now nearly 3 a.m. There was a sentry at this point who hadn't seen the colonel for about half an hour and had no idea where he might be at the moment. At last we found him in one of the buildings with the adjutant Captain J. Ford-Smith and Captain Ramsden, OC C Coy where they were snatching a few minutes sleep.

The colonel was completely unaware of the true situation and was under the impression that all companies of the Leicesters and two of the Foresters were in forward positions. In fact the whole of B Coy and about fourteen men of A Coy and thirty of C Coy were forward. All B Coy officers and all A Coy officers still alive were forward. The situation was serious indeed as it was a foregone conclusion that the enemy would continue his advance that day. The exact position in the hills of B Coy was not quite clear to the colonel and so Captain Ramsden and myself were sent out to search for them, while the adjutant and Captain Coleman, the battalion intelligence officer, were sent back to Tretten to get as many troops as possible sent forward again and to find out from Brigadier Morgan exactly what was to be done. After a search in the hills on the east for nearly an hour, we returned without having seen a trace of B Coy, but we did come across a lost party of eighteen or so of C Coy that Captain Ramsden sent down to report to the colonel at the garage buildings. When we returned, the colonel had organised a defensive position just behind the wooden buildings astride the road and was constructing a roadblock.

After distributing some food which we found there, we settled down patiently to wait and observe. Presently, Major Garner came forward up the road followed by B Coy. He had been unable to get to his position up in the hills owing to the ravines and steep gradients between the road and his would-be position. At the same time Lt Col King-Salter came forward and gave his report as to what was happening in the rear. A position (Tolstad) was to be held half-way between Tretten and the present forward position where we now were, with B Coy on the left in the hills in the original position allotted to them. The most satisfactory route to this position was to retire three miles or so before starting up into the hills. King-Salter promised to take Major Garner back and show him exactly where this position was and how to get to it. Also, all other available troops were to be sent forward. Meanwhile the forward position had to be held.

At about 9 a.m. the CO sent me back to Tretten on a bicycle which I had obtained to discover when more troops would arrive forward. I had barely gone three miles when I met Captain Coleman and a Forester MO walking forward. The former had a written message from the adjutant to the CO and having obtained as much information as possible, I returned to the CO with the message. Some troops had been sent forward and a meal was also being sent forward. A secondary position was being prepared at Tretten; as many of the dispersed troops of the Leicesters were being collected together for a final stand against the Germans. Colonel Ford and some Foresters had gone forward to the next defensive position to place themselves on the right of B Coy of the Leicesters. Such were the main contents of the message.

The CO then sent me back again to Tretten to find Brigade HQ and discover when and if this forward position was to be vacated; also any other information available. I proceeded some two miles on my bicycle and then with the help of two people who were carrying rations forward, took a motorcycle from the back of a derelict lorry and by good fortune managed to get the thing started. It was not long before the remaining five miles or so were covered and I was in Tretten where I immediately saw the adjutant, who told me all he knew. He had apparently sent a previous message up to the CO via 2nd Lt Speak and it later transpired that he and all the men with him were placed on the right flank of B Coy by King-Salter while on their way forward to the CO's Position, with the exception of a section of the Bren-carrier Platoon who were detailed to climb the hill on the east bank to guard against ski troops who might outflank the Tretten defences. The adjutant was unable to put me in touch with Brigade HQ. He informed me that besides B Coy of the Leicesters, the worn-out remnants of B and C Coys of the Foresters and 2nd Lt Speak, with a fair number of HQ personnel of the Leicesters and all available miscellaneous personnel, were in a secondary position at Tretten under Major Atkins. A Coy of the Foresters was also to be sent forward to the intermediate position at Rindheim (Map 6) on the east bank of the Laagen and just south of Tretten bridge. The west side of the bridge was to be held by D Foresters only.

On going forward to inform the CO of this, I met King-Salter. He showed me the exact dispositions of the troops on his map. I asked him if he knew when the CO was going to retire from his forward position, and his reply was that it was up to Col German to decide, but presumably when it was no longer feasible to hold it. I then proceeded forward again and met the CO about a mile behind his original forward position. It appeared that he withdrew some three hundred yards away from the original position in case of shelling, and within minutes of having done so, the forward position and the garage buildings were heavily shelled by 100 mm mortar bombs. Thereafter, the CO and some thirty men of C Coy and three officers with another fourteen men were gradually retiring. I took up my position with rifle beside the CO and told him all I knew but I realised this was where our lost field telephone equipment would have been invaluable to all concerned.

It was not long before the advance guard of enemy infantry appeared round the corner into the straight road about three hundred yards away. When they were properly into the straight the CO gave the order to open fire and a Bren gun and several riflemen scattered the enemy. The CO then ordered me to go back to Tretten and inform them there that he was retiring to the intermediate position in face of the enemy advance. This I did, taking Major German with me on the back of the motorcycle. I then collected nine volunteers with three Bren guns as a patrol to go forward and to relieve the CO. I took the motorcycle forward with a lorry load of the troops following up as far as where the intermediate place Rindheim came down to the road. Here we debussed and advanced forward on each side of the road; two Bren guns in front and one behind, in case the enemy should have got through the forest on the east side of the road and should attack us from the rear. There was always the possibility that the CO and his party might be completely cut off in a similar way.

After advancing for quarter of an hour or so we passed 2nd Lt Musson and about a hundred and twenty personnel of A Coy with an anti-tank rifle, who informed us that the CO was some way further forward but still retiring. After advancing for over half an hour, we came across the CO and his party. Captain Ramsden had been killed and one or two others wounded. He explained he was retiring as slowly as possible in order to delay the enemy as much as he could. He then left me in charge and made his way back to Rindheim to see what was happening there and to see if he could find Col Ford, CO of the Foresters.

After remaining there for some time, one or two of the enemy started shouting words of command or information, from one side of the river to the other. Eventually, when one of the enemy not far away, and almost parallel to us on the other side, he started shouting to some others who were in front of our position but below the road and in the trees between the river and the road. It looked as if it was about time to be moving again, for we had little option; our rifle ammunition was running low with no prospects of obtaining any more.

2nd Lts Kirk and Adcock and their C Coy followers therefore withdrew and went right back to the intermediate position at Rindheim, leaving only a volunteer patrol. Having given them sufficient time to get well on their way the patrol party started to withdraw in two sections, one covering the withdrawal of the other. After going about a quarter of a mile all personnel were sent straight back to the intermediate position except four people to man two Bren guns, one crew to cover the retreat of the other. The possibility of the enemy getting through the forest above the road and cutting the whole party off seemed to me to make it advisable to get as many men back to the next properly defended position where the enemy could not break through on the left, and to leave only a minimum to cover their withdrawal.

The two Bren gun crews withdrew steadily and after about twenty minutes or so, we came across Sergeant Millington of the Bren-carrier Platoon, the Leicesters, who had backed a lorry up the road in order to get us back. In a few more minutes we were at the intermediate position, where Captain Coleman placed all available personnel into the right flank of this position. The CO and Coleman on a lorry and myself on the motorcycle then returned to Tretten to discover any available news. I was never quite clear whether or not the CO had managed to contact Col Ford. It was about this time, around 3 p.m., that the enemy started shelling from behind the hills to the west of the River Laagen. The forest to the west of Tretten was heavily shelled. This was thought to be a 150 mm Howitzer. We arrived in Tretten in the vicinity of the hotel, some four hundred yards north of the bridge. Captain Coleman and I then set off to find a telephone to ring up the staff captain on receipt of a message from the latter requiring an immediate call to be put through. On the way we passed the Norwegian High Command Staff in a house and while we were having a word with them, Brigadier Morgan drove up in a car. We took him to where Col German was having a bite to eat.

A conference was to be held at 148 Brigade HQ, some half a mile north of Tretten at 4 p.m. and I accompanied the CO and the brigade commander up to the house. The Norwegian staff were there also and Colonel Jensen, CO of the Norwegian Dragoons, whose troops were operating on the left flank of the intermediate position. By 5 p.m., high level bombers began to give the Tretten area a pounding and a plan was formulated for a general withdrawal to take place as soon as it was safe to do so without the continual threat of air attack. Fresh and experienced troops were to hold a position at Ringebu (Map 1b) some sixteen miles north of Tretten, and the remnants of the two British battalions were to withdraw through them and take up a new position a further five miles north up a valley at right angles to the main Gudbrands Dalen. The withdrawal was to commence at 9 p.m.; troops under the command of Col Ford in the intermediate position were to come out first, followed by D Coy of the Foresters from the west of Tretten bridge at 10 p.m.

Only one platoon of D Coy was left here, as the remaining two platoons were taken out and sent forward to the intermediate position on the east bank of the river. But they never got there, owing to the enemy breakthrough and so the platoon left on the west side of the bridge were cut off by the enemy. Finally, the troops under Major Atkins in the Tretten position were to come out at 10.20 p.m. Transport was to be provided by the Norwegians and assembled at a place still to be agreed and notified to OC's troops. The Norwegian Dragoons with their own transport higher up in the hills were to start withdrawing about 7 p.m.

After all arrangements had been made, I was detailed to go forward and pass these withdrawal instructions to Col Ford about 4.30 p.m. I found Captain Ford-Smith, the adjutant, and gave him all the details and asked him to notify D Coy of the Foresters and Major Atkins. I then procured my motorcycle which had been refilled with petrol and went forward. I passed Major Atkins and told him briefly the plan; I also came across the RSM who had come on the patrol earlier in the day and I asked him what was happening. He said that German tanks had appeared on the road and as no further orders had been received he decided to get back to Tretten. Three-quarters of a mile forward of the Tretten position a roadblock was being prepared by a mixed party under the direction of King-Salter. It was impossible to proceed further on the motorcycle and from all accounts this would have been most unwise. German tanks had come well forward to recce and had then retired again.

I proceeded to walk forward, with a Forester officer, Brian Bradley and King-Salter who wanted to see the front line. We each had a rifle and proceeded cautiously in single file down the road. All was well for the first ten minutes or so when suddenly we were machine-gunned from the west side of the river. We took cover amongst the trees and proceeded forward. Firing was heard in front of us for some time. Coming into sight of the road again after rounding a little knoll, there down in the road not forty yards away were lorry loads of the enemy. Three tanks had gone forward and could be seen 2–300 yards behind us on the way to Tretten. The enemy had now got well behind us and the road to the right of us was swarming with them. We lay absolutely flat for ten minutes or so wondering what to do, when a 100 mm mortar started firing not fifty yards in front of us. After it had been firing for a bit, we decided to stalk it and see if we could put as many of its crew as possible out of action. King-Salter was the first to move

Lt Col King-Salter, Capt. Barratt and Lt Bradley withdrawing to Tretten from Tolstad.

and he was immediately spotted by a German from the road, who raised the hue and cry; bullets and hand grenades came hurtling at us and we withdrew further up into the forest returning rifle fire. The Forester officer, Brian Bradley, who had gone rather further forward was hit, but King-Salter and myself got well up into the wood. We decided it was useless to go further forward as the intermediate position at Rindheim must by now have been broken completely and so we decided to get back to Tretten. From the sound of it a very fierce battle was going on at Tretten. When we eventually got out, the firing seemed to be coming from a little further north, suggesting that the enemy had got through the Tretten defences. After about 6 p.m., the firing had diminished considerably and was only spasmodic, but air attack still continued. The few shots that were exchanged could be heard coming from well north of Tretten and in the dusk several houses and part of the forest round the village were seen to be well ablaze. A heavy smoke hung over the valley. The battle of Tretten was over.

After the battle of Tretten, I became completely separated from the rest of the troops. Suffice to say that I owe my life to two people – one of these, King-Salter, is mentioned several times in 'The Naked Soldiers' and it was he who extricated me from the Germans at the time that Lieutenant Bradley of the Foresters was killed. The other person was 2nd Lt Parry of the Foresters who subsequently piloted me across country and mountains to the Swedish/Norwegian frontier. After a few days there being well looked after by the Swedes, we were sent to the internment camp at Falun. Eventually, there were collected about two hundred and thirty members of all arms, including the Merchant Navy. The Swedes were very hospitable and through contact with the British Legation in Stockholm, we were supplied with English books and other reading material.

In the autumn of 1940 we were repatriated in two sections back to the UK. I was with the first section of about a hundred and twenty and we travelled north by train and coach from Falun to Petsamo in the very north of Finland. There we embarked on a Finnish ship with a Swedish captain and sailed around North Cape and eventually made landfall at Lerwick in the Shetlands. We were all subjected to the severest security restrictions until we reached the Aldershot area for debriefing. My recollections of the events of early 1940 were that the Norwegian Government was not willing to jeopardise its neutrality until it was too late. At the same time, the Allies were desperate to do whatever was possible to prevent King Haakon from falling into enemy hands. This might explain much of the chaos prevailing over embarkation problems with our troops at the various northern ports. But even the rescuing of King Haakon and his country's gold bullion didn't justify the gross mistreatment of Britain's young soldiers in sending them to a strange frozen country with inadequate clothing and grossly inadequate equipment to protect them from the enemy. Then of course came the cover up; the shambles of Norway was pushed into the background in view of the much greater shambles to come in a few days time – that of Dunkirk.

Just before Captain R. Barratt wrote this diary he had been assistant adjutant of the 1/5 Battalion, the Leicestershire Regiment during the Norwegian campaign of April 1940.

SEVEN

THE BRITISH WITHDRAW FROM NORWAY

After many requests by Brigadier Morgan for aircraft support, which had fallen on deaf ears in Whitehall, Brigadier Smythe of 15 Brigade, who was about to go into action at Kvam, also sent urgent telegrams to London, asking for air support. This time, he was going to be lucky – he was going to be given air support.

Somewhere out in the Norwegian sea about one hundred and fifty miles off the north coast, the aircraft carrier HMS *Glorious* steamed in readiness for the call to action. Her aircraft were mainly RAF Gloster Gladiators. There were problems. The starter trolleys for starting the engines could not be used as the batteries were new and uncharged and no acid had been sent with them, and the ground staff included only one armourer to maintain some seventy Browning machine-guns.

Such was the position when Squadron Leader J.W. Donaldson took off in a snowstorm from the deck of *Glorious* leading eighteen Gladiators, the pilots of which had never been in action before, and escorted by two Skuas of the Fleet Air Arm.

They descended on Lake Lesjaskog some twenty miles north of Dombaas at about 6 p.m. on 25 April without serious mishap.

The night was bitterly cold and when daylight came, the aircraft controls and the carburettors were frozen stiff and in the absence of battery trolleys the engines were difficult to get going. It was nearly two hours after first light when the first of the Gladiators took off to protect the landing ground from air attack and although one Heinkel tried it on, he was shot down; the others succeeded in dropping some bombs on the frozen lake.

At about 7 a.m. the following morning two aircraft were sent to patrol the battle area at Kvam, while the servicing party was still struggling to get more engines started. The main enemy onslaught began an hour or so later.

The Heinkel bombers approached in threes which broke formation as they came up to the target to bomb and machine-gun the lake from various heights. At least five Gladiators were destroyed before they could get off the ground, but two rose to meet the first big attack.

Altogether, some forty fighter sorties were carried out during the day in which pilots engaged the same number of enemy planes and shot down at least six and damaged several others. As the day wore on, enemy dive bombers were brought up and by late afternoon the lake was almost unusable as the Stukas' bombs broke up the runway. By this time, 27 April, only four serviceable aircraft remained apart from Squadron Leader Donaldson's and it was decided to withdraw from Lesjaskog to a landing ground near Aandalsnes.

On this day, three aircraft patrolled the landing ground at Setnesmoen, the fourth acted as a recce aircraft in the Dombaas/Otta area, reporting troop movements to Sickleforce HQ, while the fifth was sent to recce Simsdal where a German landing had been reported, but its engine failed completely and the pilot had to bale out. By nightfall three more Gladiators were rendered unserviceable on account of damage which there was no means of repairing. The remaining aircraft was not flown again so the British attempt to base much needed fighters in central Norway was abandoned.

The Air Ministry in its wisdom felt it was unable to accede to General Paget's request for heavy bombers to attack the enemy because the targets were out of range.

We left Brigadier Smythe of 15 Brigade on the morning of 25 April with his troops deployed in the Kvam position.

They did not have to wait long. An enemy column approached the bend without warning at about 11 a.m. An anti-tank gun located on the island opened fire and scored a hit, for both tanks stopped and the armoured car withdrew back round the bend.

Enemy infantry at once deployed on both sides of the road and their close support guns were brought into action causing considerable casualties.

By 4 p.m. the advance company, having lost four officers and eighty-five other ranks, was forced to fall back about half a mile to the western end of the island, where a second company was positioned.

The enemy tried to outflank our other forward position, but our men, who were well dug in there, carried out considerable slaughter amongst the enemy forces, and at about 5 p.m., the arrival of a company of the Yorks and Lancs enabled this front to be extended up the hillside to the rear of our original position.

A second enemy tank advanced slowly forward but a shell from one of the anti-tank guns smashed its track and immobilised it, causing it to block the road.

Another enemy attempt to push on up the river in rubber dinghies was equally unsuccessful as the Koylis shot up the dinghies and sank them. By nightfall the battalion was holding all its original positions, except for the eastern part of the island. The enemy, as was his usual practice, made no movement during the night.

Early next morning, 26 April, fighting was renewed at Kvam with a heavy artillery barrage, then about 6.30 a.m. the enemy attacked on the left flank in battalion strength but was held.

At this point, enemy aircraft and an additional battery of artillery were brought into action. This enabled the enemy to close in on our position and establish machine-gun nests at close range.

At about 2 p.m. a tank succeeded in advancing up the road towards Kvam under cover of the screen established for our own protection against the machine-guns. A volunteer removed the screen under fire and one of our anti-tank guns went into action at about one thousand yards and set fire to this and a second tank; though the anti-tank gun itself was destroyed a few minutes later.

The position was becoming serious as enemy infiltration occurred at various points and threatened to cut off our companies from each other. On our left flank, they advanced down a side road, which meets the main road at right angles behind the village. Fortunately, a platoon guarding the rear of a forward company on the flank restored the situation at about 4 p.m., inflicting a number of casualties on the enemy.

The enemy were also harassed in this area by ski troops of the Norwegian Second Division. At about 5 p.m., the Koylis and a company of the Yorks and Lancs battalion were withdrawn on the orders of General Paget. About this time the enemy reverted to his old tricks of setting fire to the woods on either side of the valley with incendiary bombs so that our position had to be abandoned some hours earlier than had been intended. The Germans did not interfere with this withdrawal, confident that the British did not pose a serious threat.

Two companies of the Koylis on the exposed flank did not get the orders to withdraw and consequently had to make their escape by long detours over the still snow-clad mountains. This was yet another example of the sort of poor communications which befell 148 Brigade earlier on.

The orders which General Paget had given to the British troops in Kvam, were founded on wider considerations besides the difficulties of their immediate position. After his first conference with Brigadier Morgan he had reported home at once that the situation was unsatisfactory. It was bound to be, for 15 Brigade still had no more equipment than 148 had, except for the seven 25 mm Hotchkiss anti-tank guns. There was still no reliable air support, no anti-tank support, no artillery and no armour. The Luftwaffe ruled supreme with no opposition. 15 Brigade were also naked soldiers, trying to oppose an estimated three enemy divisions with supporting artillery and armour, and yet in spite of General Paget's efforts to get the situation across to his superiors, the following day brought a message from General Massy emphasising the importance of not only securing a bridgehead to include Dombaas, but the next forty miles north on the road to Trondheim as far as Opdal so that a second base might be established.

Such a base was to provide for a build-up of strong forces which would include the French Chasseurs des Alpines, who were just as badly equipped as we were and had no skis.

The failure to establish a fighter squadron on Lake Lesjaskog was not at this stage known at home. All the British public were told was that everything was going 'according to plan'. The complete rout of 148 Brigade was referred to as a strategic withdrawal.

By 26 April, the Germans had advanced up the Osterdahl to Tynset and Roros and southwards from Trondheim as far as Storen. Roros had changed hands several times but on 27th further information showed that the enemy had sent a force up another side valley towards Hjerkinn (Map 1b)which meant they would shortly be in a position to cut the Dombaas/Opdal route only about twenty miles north of Dombaas.

This enemy group comprised Army Group Fischer and was made up of a mountain regiment, a parachute group and at least three battalions of infantry, supported by more tanks than Group Pellengahr, which we faced further south. So whilst we were facing south down the Gudbrandsdal, we were now threatened on our flank in the rear. Such an approach towards the Dombaas area could cut off most of our forces further down the valley.

Because of this threat on 27 April, General Paget set out by car to reconnoitre the Dombaas/Opdal road as far as Hjerkinn but failed to get through the deep snow. Another recce was made on the following day which brought news from the Norwegians that there had been no contact with the enemy in that area.

Meanwhile, the action which had been broken off by the British troops at Kvam had been renewed at Kjorem. It was not thought that the enemy could be held for more than a day. The Green Howards were therefore ordered to prepare a second position at Otta and Brigadier Morgan reconnoitred a third position in front of Dombaas on the afternoon of 27th to provide for the possibility of a hurried withdrawal. Here, the Green Howards, reinforced by the remnants of the 148 Brigade, would make a stand and form a rearguard for the forward troops. General Paget's main object was to hang on at Dombaas pending the arrival of the reinforcements he had asked for.

At Kjorem, the road and railway still ran north-westwards along the left bank of the Laagen, but the valley floor is narrower. The position of the Yorks and Lancs Battalion astride the road had been well dug in and troops were deployed in advance of it on both banks of the river with standing patrols at a considerable height amongst the trees, broken ground and occasional farm buildings on the hillside.

At about 8 a.m. on 27 April, the enemy approached up the road and were engaged with some success from across the river. They then brought up machine-guns and 100 mm mortars not only along the road, but also on the right bank of the river, by which means they were able to subject both flanks of the cover position to crossfire. This position was protected by conifer trees which the Germans succeeded in setting fire to with incendiary mortar bombs. On this occasion, we also had a 3 in mortar in action, but it was not very effective. The blazing trees caused one company to withdraw and when they counter-attacked, the enemy had already secured their position with tanks and machine-guns. A new line was established a short distance west of the hamlet of Kjorem and this was held until nightfall. Our troops on the right bank of the Laagen were now exposed to crossfire at close quarters and although the enemy advance along that bank met with little success, by 6 p.m. the crossfire had compelled a further withdrawal from our advanced position, and at about 10 p.m. the last troops on the right bank went back to cross the river higher up. At about 11 p.m. withdrawal began on the west bank as well. They re-established a roadblock in our rear and from it they now opened fire with heavy machine-guns at short range.

At Otta next morning, the strength of the battalion had fallen to thirteen officers and about 300 men. The equivalent of one more company from the right bank, having missed the river crossing and wandered into the Heidal, arrived at Dombaas twenty-four hours later.

Now it was the turn of the Green Howards. They were short of one company which was now made up from the remnants of 148 Brigade protecting Dombaas. A second company, which had served on the right flank of the Yorks and Lancs the previous day, sustained serious losses.

Two steeply rising spurs of land on the hillside, one on the left bank about one and a half miles in front of the town, the other on the right much nearer in with sheltered access from the side valley, gave scope for effective crossfire and would be very hard to storm. Each spur was held by one company and the rest of the troops were posted in and behind the town where the five surviving anti-tank guns were also sited. An evening on reconnaissance by the Germans was followed up at about 7 a.m. on the 28th by an air attack which did very little damage. At about 10.30 a.m., about 150 enemy with tanks and artillery advanced against our right flank. Heavy casualties were inflicted on them, whereupon they deployed to both flanks. Their artillery was then brought into action against whatever target that could be located.

Tanks were again employed on both banks. On the right bank they had very little room to manoeuvre and on the left where they came along the road, a single anti-tank gun knocked out three in succession. Another party of the enemy were surprised while crossing the river in rubber dinghies to attack our forward positions and suffered further casualties.

Lt Col German CO of 1/5 Leicesters when taken prisoner at Venabygd, north of Tretten.

Several small actions were fought by the company protecting the most distant spur, in one of which some thirty members of a German officers conference were surprised and disposed of. By evening the company occupied a higher post on the hillside backing onto the foot of a precipice. From there it pinned down enemy detachments almost twice its own strength.

General Paget gave orders for a withdrawal to begin at 10 p.m. when the forward company from the right bank crossed the River Otta by a ford, after the railway bridge leading to the town had been blown up.

Heavy fire was concentrated on the area which we had just abandoned, but a general retirement from the town began after the disablement of our remaining anti-tank guns was carried out by the Green Howards and the Yorks and Lancs in the rear. The advance company, in its strong but isolated position on the left bank, did not receive the order to withdraw and at about 10.30 p.m. drove off a superior force of the enemy and suffered heavy losses. It then divided into four parties which moved back in silence and for the most part, on hands and knees at a height of well over one thousand feet above the valley floor along a precipitous slope, and arrived at the town at about 6 a.m. to find that their battalion had left. The company was still almost complete in numbers and arms and although fired on by enemy snipers in Otta, suffered no loss as it set out on its 39 mile march up the valley to Dombaas. The break away this time had been complete and the enemy made no attempt to follow.

But now, the General was faced with the difficult task of extricating his troops along a narrow valley route.

As the Germans advanced up the Gudbrandsdal, they followed the usual blitzkrieg tactics of bombing villages and towns which lay in their path to make it easier for their troops to take over without a lot of house-to-house fighting. 'Flatten everything' was the Luftwaffe's policy. On or about 26 April, Aandalsnes began to get this type of treatment from the Luftwaffe and persistent raids very quickly set fire to the wooden quay, various stores and the lower part of the town.

While morale was at a low ebb, the situation was made worse by the fact that the Germans now began high-altitude bombing which put their aircraft well out of range of anti-aircraft artillery. Our communications received a setback by the bombing of Molde, which destroyed the electric power supply knocking out the Norwegian wireless transmitter which could no longer be used to communicate with England.

On 27th, Aandalsnes had several more raids between 11 a.m. and

A view of the town of Aandalsnes on fire, from the Romsdal Fjord.

4 p.m. in which rations, demolition stores, ammunition and explosives were lost. This same afternoon a supply convoy of ships entered the fjord but left again soon afterwards under strengthened escort with the greater part of a heavy anti-tank battery, the first to reach Norway, still on board.

On 28th, when 15 Brigade was still resisting the German advance at Otta, two messages reached General Paget from the base at Aandalsnes. They advised him that ships would be available on the nights of 30 April/1 May and men were to be got away regardless of loss of equipment.

Paget was still of the opinion that he could hold Dombaas area for a time if further landings were planned and if air and artillery support could be provided at once. His chief concern though, was how the Norwegians would react.

Meanwhile at Aandalsnes, it was obvious that the Luftwaffe had set out to destroy the whole town with constant air raids and although the joint efforts of anti-aircraft cruisers and sloops in the fjord gave some temporary relief, the destruction went on remorselessly.

The *Black Swan* fired some 2,000 rounds of four-inch shells and more than twice that amount of pompom ammunition in two days, then left the scene of battle for Scapa Flow with a three-foot bomb hole in the hull below the water line.

The withdrawal of the troops became a problem for General Paget, not only of his own, but those of the Norwegian 2nd Division and Dahl Force under Col Dahl. Another problem was the single railway line and the one and only road to the coast. Both the railway and the road, which were bombed daily, were miraculously repaired by Norwegian civilians almost as soon as they were damaged.

Both railway and road ran together, which presented an easy target for enemy planes to wreak maximum destruction.

At this particular time there was practically no communication between 15 Brigade and the base at Aandalsnes. However, they were still able to organise the details of their retirement by the use of civil telephones, but in the latter stages were left entirely dependent on motor cycle despatch riders using the single road.

Once evacuation had been decided on, 15 Brigade's first task was to break off contact with the enemy. At about 6 p.m. on 28 April, the KOYLI was ordered to occupy a position south of Dombaas rail junction.

The remnants of our own battalion and that of the Sherwood Foresters which had made up 148 Brigade, about 150 men and three officers, were assembled at Dombaas station at about 8 p.m. on that day. They faced a forced march along the railway track back to Aandalsnes.

Major German told us that we faced a sixty mile march to get back to the port. The Leicesters would be split up into three groups with himself at the head, Captain Hobbins with the second group and Lt QM Sid

Morson at the head of the third group. There would be no stopping for ten minutes' break in every hour.

At about 11 p.m. after we had gone, a train was assembled by the Norwegians along with some motor transport for the remainder of 15 Brigade and a successful withdrawal began.

By daylight, about 3 a.m., the troops from the front line were in Dombaas covered by the KOYLI. As the British forces made their withdrawal, a section of Royal Engineers exploded demolition charges in the wild Rosti gorge where the road bridge crosses onto the right bank of the river and at a railway bridge further back towards Dombaas.

General Ruge had made it plain that the Norwegian detachment which had been protecting our flanks from the Opdal wouldn't reach Dombaas until the night of 29 April, so that the British withdrawal had to be postponed until the night of 30th and the town had to be held for another forty-eight hours. This task would have been given to the one hundred and fifty remnants of 148 Brigade but it was now too late as they had departed on 28th, so that the neighbourhood of Dombaas was left unguarded except for the anti-tank company, which now had no guns.

The day of 29th passed according to plan at Dombaas with the troops resting in positions well concealed from German air observation. The last Norwegian detachment passing through the town from Hjerkinn and the 1st Yorks and Lancs left by about 10 p.m.

On the afternoon of 30th, the KOYLI, from their position three miles south of the town, saw the Germans advancing up the road. They were on foot and using handcarts to carry mortars and ammunition.

They were taken by surprise when our troops attacked them, supported by four Norwegian field guns on the hillside behind Dombaas. The Germans suffered very heavy casualties.

It was noticed that when the enemy had no air or artillery support, our own troops were not only able to hold them but able to adopt an aggressive attitude.

The Germans were held in check by the Green Howards who had been guarding the approach to Dombaas from Hjerkinn. The main bulk of these troops got away from Dombaas in the last train which left about 11.30 p.m. on 29th for Aandalsnes. The two rear companies followed in trucks half an hour later.

Everything now depended on the condition of the railway ahead, which had been subjected to heavy bombing, and with the completion of the Norwegian withdrawal and that of the remnants of 148 Brigade, there was no further need to protect or repair it. The train which carried the Yorks and Lancs about an hour earlier, had been halted by a break in the rails at Lesjaskog. What remained of the battalion had to continue its journey on foot. The line was reported to be in working order again at about 5 p.m. on 30th. No one anticipated the accident which followed.

The train had picked up about 280 Norwegian ski troops and the anti-tank company and was travelling westwards towards Aandalsnes when both engines overturned and the front coach was telescoped at a bomb crater east of Lesjaskog. There were eight fatal and many serious casualties.

The whole area was deep in snow, being almost 3,000 feet above sea level and there was no cover either from air attack or to provide any other defence. The uninjured set out to march to Verma, seventeen miles west, while some vehicles were brought forward to pick up the injured. They were attacked by enemy aircraft on the way but managed to reach the safety of the Verma tunnel by about 10 p.m. on 30th.

The Verma tunnel, which adjoins the station, is almost five hundred yards long and provided perfect air cover for the resting troops. It also provided cover for various stores.

Enemy bombers tried in vain to block the entrance and exit to the tunnel with bombs but failed to do so. Meanwhile a party of Royal Marines had been hurried forward to cover the scene of the accident and to give protection for the troops on the march from being overrun by an enemy advance from Dombaas.

At this time, a company of the Green Howards was deployed about three miles up the road and at about 7 p.m. on 30 April, a small Lewis gun detachment of marines came through. The last train eventually left about 8 p.m. carrying the main body of troops and just over a company of Green Howards along with a few marines which had formed the last rearguard and which followed in trucks.

After the trucks had departed, a small party of Sherwood Foresters with Corporal George Templeman in charge, approached the Verma tunnel in the hope of getting some transport to the base. Here, apparently, they were intercepted by an officer who introduced himself as General Carton de Wiart of 146 Brigade which was based on Namsos, nearly 200 miles further north. He gave orders to set up a guard on the tunnel to protect the supplies and then left. Templeman and his comrades wondered if it was in fact de Wiart so far from his own base?

But the Foresters knew that the enemy were not far away and they had very few rounds of rifle ammunition left with which to defend themselves. They also discovered that there was no more transport and their only hope was to walk. They set off through the woods and had not gone far when they discovered an abandoned lorry by the side of the road. They were able to get it going and make it back to Aandalsnes where they were taken aboard HMS *Birmingham*.

But what were the fortunes of 146 Brigade, designated Mauriceforce? Originally bound for Narvik, but redirected to Namsos to march on

Trondheim and link up with 148 Brigade marching north from Dombaas. Sergeant George Andrews of the 1/4th Lincolnshire Regiment now tells us of events leading up to this impossible dream:

> We landed with the first group at Namsos. Here, we were billeted in a school overnight and the following morning moved south towards Steinkjer. (Map 2)
>
> I was with a section who were detailed to mount our Bren guns on tripods in a woodyard at the edge of the town overlooking Beitstad fjord in case German ships came up the fjord from Trondheim, which they did later and landed troops between us and the forward companies. From then on things got rather hot. A German cruiser came up the fjord, fired a few shells and then went back, nobody knew why. Later, we had to transport some prisoners who had been taken from a ship that had been trapped in the ice on the edge of the fjord during the night.
>
> It was about this time that German high-level bombers arrived and bombed Steinkjer flat. One of the first bombs dropped blew the end out of the store shed we were in and the shed caught fire. We decided it was time to get out of there.
>
> We moved up the hillside through about two feet of snow onto a truck and found that we were more or less on a level with the planes bombing the town. Once or twice we thought of using our Brens on the planes bombing the town, but decided against it for the magazines we had left were loaded with tracer bullets which would have not only given our position away but endangered the lives of hundreds of refugees moving through our position.
>
> We finally joined up with a few more of our platoon and slept out on the hillside among the conifer trees. When we awoke we felt shattered and absolutely frozen stiff, some of the Platoon suffered from frostbite as a result of this. We moved off again in the evening on the long trek back to Namsos, staying briefly in barns and villages and moving on in the two or three hours of twilight which passed as night-time and so avoided the machine-gunning from fighter aircraft, but this didn't always work.
>
> I remember one farm, still intact, where some of us holed up overnight. The farmer let us sleep in his hayloft. Some of us moved out after it was bombed and took up positions under some conifers near the farmhouse but the heat from the burning building was melting the snow around us. Those of us who were left pushed on and joined up with more of our unit who were moving along the road on the far side of an open space and resumed our trek to Namsos. Just before reaching Namsos, one of our trucks came along, the only one I'd seen since we left Steinkjer, with some enemy prisoners. They weren't army personnel and one was only a young boy of no more than fifteen years of age who had an Alsatian dog with him. Myself and a L/Cpl Peacock were

138

taken aboard the truck as guards and on to Namsos, which was also in ruins.

Here we stayed in one of the few remaining undamaged houses and at this stage we had no food left, so myself and 'Tiny' Peacock, he was over six foot tall, went out into the wrecked town to see what we could find by way of food; the civilians had all gone by this time, but all we found were a few tins of soup and some dry biscuits. Tiny got a fire going and made the soup, then a lone German fighter plane which had seen the smoke from the fire we lit came into attack us. Nobody was badly hurt but the big bowl of soup that Tiny had made was overturned onto the ground. Now Tiny, who was scared of nothing, rushed outside and waved his fist at the disappearing plane, shouting 'You rotten bugger, you've ruined our lunch.'

Eventually we boarded the destroyer *Afridi* in the early hours of the morning, but we had to get off further up the fjord and board another ship called the *El Quantara*, which after incessant bombing in the fjord, took us to Scapa Flow where we transferred to the *Reina del Pacifico*. We lost more ships in the convoy coming back from Norway and I have learned since that the *Afridi* was holed by a bomb in the fjord and several people were killed by the blast.

I must make a special mention of Major Stokes, our company commander, as he came to see me in hospital later. I had damage to my left hand and left eye. I was downgraded and transferred to another unit and promoted to Sergeant and finished my last years of service i/c prisoner of war camp at St. Teath in Cornwall.

Private Bert Atkin served in the Yorks & Lancs (Hallamshire Regiment) as part of 146 Brigade and tells of his experiences:

My part in the event was not all that heroic. I joined the battalion on the quayside at Gourock on 8 April, 1940.

We sailed on the Polish ship *Chrobry* bound for Narvik, or so I was told, and on 11th, whilst at sea, we were told that Narvik had been taken by the Germans, so we were diverted to Namsos.

The original plan saw the Hallamshires peacefully occupying and garrisoning Norway, but even as they sailed, events overtook the plan when three specially trained German divisions attacked Norway. To make matters worse, Lt Col Robbins the officer commanding the Hallamshires was unable to discuss the operation in detail with the commander of 146 Brigade or the other two battalions for all were sailing on board different ships.

On 16 April, the Hallamshires transport entered the Namsen fjord and the battalion transferred to three destroyers, HMS *Nubian*, *Matabele* and *Mashorba* under continuous enemy air attack which caused no casualties.

Low cloud and snow saved us. It was a very scary experience for green soldiers like me. By chance the Hallamshires took over their new locations from the Royal Marine detachment of the cruiser HMS *Sheffield* which had landed some twenty hours previously as an advance guard.

We landed at Namsos quay at about 11 p.m. and my platoon was sent to guard the far end of a bridge. There was about three to four feet of snow all around and it was not very pleasant. Next morning we moved on to Follafoss Power station, well in advance of Coy HQ and on the opposite side of the fjord from the rest of the battalion. Here we felt very isolated but had good positions under cover with good fields of fire on the road and across the fjord. There were good cooking facilities and dry beds. There was no restriction on movement except when enemy reconnaissance aircraft were around. Ammunitionwise, there were 200 rounds per Bren gun of which we had three, and fifty 303 rounds per man. There was one two inch mortar but no bombs for it and one Boyes anti-tank rifle which became my responsibility. We felt very confident.

The brigade objective was Steinkjer, some 120 miles away and it had no artillery, no air support, no access to Naval gunfire support and no transport. Radios were almost non-existent and the KOYLI had none at all. Strict radio silence was imposed and all stores were hurriedly camouflaged. These measures were successful for the Germans didn't know we had landed until about four days later.

On the night of 17 April, the Hallamshires embussed and made a rapid advance of some sixty miles towards Trondheim. The Hallamshires then secured a forward defensive position which allowed the two other battalions of the brigade to leapfrog through by train.

Meanwhile, my platoon, which had been left behind on the opposite side of the Beitstad fjord, sighted two enemy armed trawlers and two launches. Were they landing behind us, we wondered, but we were told to wait and see. Things began to get somewhat tense, for Namsos was well and truly bombed that night and we could see a glow in the sky behind us. Our battalion stores were destroyed in this raid and it would be goodbye to all the gear I signed for. The next day a German destroyer and a cargo ship were sighted in the fjord and there were sounds of firing across the fjord. Would this have been the Lincolns, we wondered?

By 20 April, 146 Brigade was over three quarters of the way towards its objective of Trondheim but its battalions were strung out over a fifty mile area of the coastline. No German ground forces had been encountered but an enemy aircraft nicknamed 'Henry the Hun' had tracked their advance throughout and this resulted in numerous attacks by the Germans.

Back in Namsos, the battalion stores which had remained undetected, were now reduced to a shambles when the town was bombed. On the following day, 21st, the Germans made use of their superior naval power by entering the fjords and landing large numbers of troops which took up positions in between the three battalions of the 146th Brigade. Considerable numbers landed behind the Koylis and the Lincolns, who were cut off, leaving the Hallamshires as the brigade front line. A Coy of the Hallamshires saw German warships landing troops on the Beitstad fjord, but were powerless to attack them, having no heavy weapons, artillery or naval gunfire to direct onto the landing enemy troops.

The Hallamshires were now in a predicament for their firm base of Namsos was now wrecked and the two other battalions of the brigade were cut off. Communications were poor and a suspected fifth column rumour soon spread that the other two battalions had been completely wiped out by large numbers of the enemy, who were even now, massing for an attack on the Hallamshires. Not all rumours were well founded. A report of machine-gun fire turned out to be civilian locals chopping firewood. A second of Germans digging a mortar position proved to be farmers digging a cow out of a snowdrift. Brigade HQ now sent orders that the Hallamshires were to withdraw towards Namsos and establish a defensive position at Folling through which the two forward battalions could pass into safety.

To get back to my platoon's position on the far side of Beitstad fjord. We watched on the night of the 22nd as Steinkjer was bombed and saw the red glow in the sky again. We were told to withdraw to Malm and found it hard going in a snowstorm which we were glad of as cover from aircraft. On this same day we were told to move to Beitstad to cover the Koylis' withdrawal. They had lost a lot of men and at this time we had no idea where the Lincolns were. Patrols were out at night to try and recover stores left behind by men taking up positions in whatever cover they could find and there was very little on Follafoss.

Far from being overrun, the Koylis had given a good account of themselves at Verdal bridge, the approaches to which were strewn with German dead from the 130th Regiment. Both forward battalions extracted themselves by a determined forced march of detour and managed to cover 58 miles in 42 hours. Although casualties had been suffered and the cross country route dictated that they leave all but their weapons behind, the forward battalions were in good order. The Sheffield accents of B Coy were music to the men of the Wakefield KOYLI and they trudged into the safety of the Hallamshire defences on the night of St George's Day.

On 26th we sent out patrols to Steinkjer and Maere to attack German positions. Two Germans were killed and one captured, the rest withdrew.

On 26th, 200 Territorials of the Lincolns also passed through the Hallamshires' front line to rejoin their battalion after all hope for them had been given up. A corporal and three men of A Coy seemed to appear from nowhere after having been given up for dead.

28 April and my birthday. For a present the French Chasseurs des Alpines relieved us and we withdrew to the outskirts of Namsos. The town

was completely destroyed and not a civilian to be seen. More snow fell and the fog in the fjord delayed the withdrawal plans. The bridge we guarded on the first night had been blown up by the REs. New orders came for the Hallamshires to withdraw from Folling and to take up a defensive position at Bagsund where the battalion was to act as rearguard whilst the brigade evacuated from Norway by sea.

The brigade embarked on the evening of 2 May, and in the early hours of 3 May after several patrols in miserable conditions of snow and no further contact with the Germans our platoon withdrew to the quay and boarded HMS *Afridi*. First to land and last to leave was Lt Col Robbins who remained at Namsos until dawn, on board HMS *Afridi*, when he and Captain Cave slipped back ashore to see that none had been left behind. Once back on board, *Afridi* sailed to join the rest of the convoy completely unaware that their departure from Norway had been broadcast in advance by the BBC. Heavy enemy air attacks followed and about 1300 hours *Afridi* was hit by a bomb and sank within twenty minutes. There was a scramble to get on deck, but no panic, for the navy was in control. Two destroyers, HMS *Griffin* and HMS *Imperial* closed in, one either side of *Afridi* and we just had to step across on to their decks and get out of their way. Thirteen members of the battalion were killed and eleven wounded in the attack. HMS *Griffin* took us back to Scapa Flow.

At about 8 p.m. on 29 April, we left the remnants of the Leicesters assembled at Dombaas station as we prepared to face the 60-odd mile march back to the base on foot.

Marching along the sleepers within the precincts of the station, where the ground between them was reasonably solid, was fairly easy, but as we left the town behind, the ballast between the sleepers became gravelly and less firm and more difficult to avoid. My long stride meant four steps on the sleepers and the fifth in the gravel.

'It's a pity these sleepers aren't a little bit further apart,' I complained.

We marched on in silence and I tried walking on the snow-covered grass beside the track, but found this was more exhausting than the sleepers. After an hour or so the strain began to tell. We marched automatically. But this state of affairs was just about to change and it was around midnight when some of my comrades began to crack up. We had begun to suffer from the effects of lack of food and unsuitable clothing. Our greatcoats were far from ideal in our present predicament, where our movements generated heat. At night, the sub-Arctic temperatures penetrated them easily and they were too long and restricted the free movement of our legs.

An important national newspaper covering the embarkation of some of our troops for Norway was said to have been impressed by the equipment of the men, which included white fur jackets, white jerseys and pullovers, fur caps and leather jerkins. What happened to this fantastic equipment is anybody's guess, it certainly wasn't issued to either 148 or 15 Brigades. The Director General of Equipment and Stores told the House that he was 'convinced that our troops in Norway are better supplied than the Germans. All our equipment is of the finest quality (like our useless anti-tank rifles) whilst the Germans have to use substitutes for many things.'

It's a pity this politician didn't go there and find out for himself that the German tanks were anything but substitutes. By the time we got to the port my feet were covered in sores and chilblains, even my fingers swelled and itched constantly.

It had now been almost a week since we had any food and although we didn't realise it as first, we just didn't have the energy for a sustained march. The first few miles had not been too bad but the combination of ballast and sleepers and lack of food began to take their toll.

It started at first with a lone voice somewhere at the rear of the column of troops, muttering something in the darkness, then gradually one after another began to join in, then several voices at the rear could be heard shouting and screaming at the major.

'For Christ's sake stop – the bloody man's a maniac.' Then another.

'I'm not going any further – I'm knackered.' Then another.

'The bloody Jerries can't be any worse than this bastard!' So it went on. Then there would be silence for a while. I looked behind me once or twice and saw some of them tearing off their overcoats and helmets and throwing them down by the side of the track regardless of the warning the major had given us about doing just this, then, as if this wasn't enough, I saw one of them throw his rifle away without even bothering to remove the bolt. I told Dunk what was going on and he quickly put my anxiety at rest.

'Don't bother about them Lofty, the silly buggers will either freeze to death tonight, or they could even be shot with their own rifles; if they won't take notice of the major, they won't take notice of anyone, so let them get on with it.'

Private Richard 'Squeek' Adams, who was marching alongside me, was beginning to show signs of faltering and stumbled once or twice. Squeek was one of the battalion buglers, hence his nickname.

'What's the matter, Squeek?' I asked him.

'It's me rifle, mate, it's getting too heavy for me, but I'm not going to part with it even if it means falling out for a rest.'

'No – don't do that, Squeek, you might not be able to get going again; give it here, I can manage it.' I said, taking his rifle and slinging it over my shoulder alongside my own.

Squeek was alright after that and was able to keep up with the rest of us. I looked back again and saw that there were more men dropping out at the rear of the column, some quietly and without any fuss, others with curses and threats.

About 2 a.m. there was another uproar from the back of the column and this time Major German halted us and made his way back down to the rear where all the commotion had been coming from, to see if he could sort out some of the problems. Some of us followed him to see what all the fuss was about. We listened as he spoke to them. All he did was reiterate what he told us at Dombaas, that the march would be long and arduous and that we had two options; to march to the coast or be captured by the enemy.

'I see some of you are without your greatcoats and steel helmets and even your best friend – your rifle.'

'What bloody good are rifles to a beaten army?' a voice wanted to know.

'We are not a beaten army,' the major snorted indignantly. 'A well ordered retreat is just as important as a strategic advance, anyway, I'm sorry you have disregarded my advice and hope you will not live to regret your actions.'

With that, the major turned back to the head of the column and once more we started off.

We plodded on silently through the semi-darkness of the Norwegian night, in silence, heeding not the beauty of the Northern Lights. My own legs functioned automatically as though they were completely cut off from my brain.

It must have been about 4 a.m. when it happened. The roar of its engines suddenly burst upon our ears from somewhere up ahead of us and to the right of us and behind a screen of trees. Then it was suddenly upon us, the black shape of a strange kind of aircraft fitted with skis. A shout from up ahead had us all diving for cover, but there was little of that.

My comrades cursed the aircraft when they discovered it was Norwegian and not the German plane they had expected.

After this episode, the major decided to try to find somewhere for us to rest up out of sight of patrolling aircraft for the remainder of the day.

After another hour of marching we came across another of those most welcome sights, a Norwegian hayloft well stocked with dry, sweet-smelling hay. Here at least, the major said, we would be out of sight of any marauding aircraft and would be in a better condition to continue our journey that night.

It was the sound of the chattering voices of my comrades that woke me up during the evening of 30 April.

The voices were interrupted by the major. 'Right, lads,' he said briefly, 'let's get on with the journey, we've still got about another forty miles or so ahead of us, but we've all had a good rest so it shouldn't take us long.'

We formed up again on the railway line and started out once more leaving behind several of our comrades who had other ideas of getting to the base port of Aandalsnes. We were very lucky, for after we had marched several more miles, we eventually arrived at the station of Lesjaskog and here we found an empty train which eventually took us on to the port. Some of my comrades had opted to make their own way: Corporal Arthur Thomas, tells us how he got there.

I saw a small group of lads trying to lift a railway trolley onto the line and me and my mate Reg Sutton decided to give them a hand and between us we got it onto the rails and we must have travelled ten or twelve miles before we ran out of track due to the bombing by enemy aircraft. I remember two other comrades CSM Keaton and Sergeant Bill Wain, who were on the bogie. We then had to continue by road for the rest of the way.

We walked for miles and eventually heard a lorry coming and managed to get a lift from a very reluctant driver. His load was the infamous Boyes anti-tank rifles in boxes with more boxes of ammunition. The load was so heavy for the lorry that when we came to a hill, we had to get out and push. This was one occasion when I became unstuck for I didn't get back into the lorry quick enough and I was left behind. Shouting after it didn't help either.

I now found myself completely alone with miles and miles of road stretching away into the distance, lines of vehicles on one side of me and not a soul in sight, but my luck was about to change and after I had walked about four miles, I caught up with the lorry which had come to a full stop for some mechanical reason.

Our own party, headed by Major German, arrived in the port in the early hours of 30 April and very quickly made for a conifer-covered hillside on the outskirts of the town overlooking the harbour where we concealed ourselves as best we could amongst the trees and boulders. But the Luftwaffe knew we were there.

For almost two days we waited patiently in the trees on the hillside above Aandalsnes, to be taken off by the Navy. We were then told by Major German that the cruiser HMS *Sheffield* had been trying unsuccessfully to get down the fjord to take us off. Several air attacks had prevented her in the limited hours of darkness from coming in too close to the wooden jetty.

By this time Aandalsnes was no longer the picturesque little town we had seen when we landed on 22 April. A thick pall of black smoke hung over the place. It was reduced to nothing but rubble.

The first day after our arrival back at the port was sheer hell. A couple of marines had been located on the shoulder of the hill somewhat higher up than where we sheltered among the conifer trees and they were armed with twin Lewis machine-guns mounted on a tripod. They were no more than about fifty yards away from us and we could see their every move quite plainly.

During the long daylight hours of that first day, we found it impossible to rest or even doze with the racket that went on around us and most of us were still exhausted from that forced march from Dombaas and were now very weak from lack of food and drink. It wasn't very long before the marines were spotted by an Me 110 which circled round the hill and it must have been about 8 a.m. when the sparks began to fly. It flew round and round the hill and each time it came opposite the marines, its gunner let fly with everything he had and they replied doggedly with their Lewis guns.

Fortunately for us, there was ample cover amongst the trees and even on the hillside there were the usual boulders lying about which provided us with extra cover. The few hours of darkness brought us little respite from the attentions of the Luftwaffe. Daylight lasted until about 11 p.m. and then a kind of dusk fell until about 3 o'clock in the morning when it started slowly to get lighter.

When I awoke shortly after about 6 a.m. the sun was well up. My mouth felt as though it was full of sawdust and I struggled to my feet to stretch my cramped and cold limbs. It was my feet that puzzled me at this particular moment for they felt so heavy and it seemed as though they were weighted down by boots similar to those of a deep sea diver.

'You alright there, Lofty?' Len Dunkley asked cheerfully from behind the shelter of a conifer.

'So far, mate,' I replied, 'But I'm having a hell of a job to move my feet and legs and my tongue feels like a piece of emery paper. Have you any water left in your bottle?'

''fraid not, Lofty – my bottle's empty.'

'Right, Len – let me have it and I'll go and fill it up at the stream.'

'What stream – there's no water round here,' he said.

'There's a stream at the bottom of the hill, I've been listening to it for ages, can't you hear it?'

'I can't hear a damned thing but I think I can hear those Jerry aeroplanes coming back; you be careful, mate, if they catch you in the open, they'll have you.'

'They'd have a job, Len,' I laughed, 'I'm that bloody thin they'd never see me.'

I took the water bottle out of Len's hand, picked up my rifle and slung it over my shoulder and picked my way carefully and somewhat painfully down the hill in the direction of the sound of babbling water.

Towards the bottom of the hill I came out of the trees and into the open and began to cross a stretch of yellowish grass-covered ground.

I had only got about halfway across this piece of open ground when two Me 110s suddenly roared towards me. The sudden noise of their engines as they came from behind the hill took me by surprise.

Their machine-guns chattered for three or four seconds and bullets zipped into the soft earth all around me, but I was too weak to pay much attention to them and I certainly felt no fear, only anger that I couldn't strike back at them, so I just stood where I was looking upwards at them helplessly as they passed overhead. But I made my feelings known by standing and shaking my empty rifle at them and cursing them roundly. My weakness had given me a new strength – I realised I'd lost all fear of danger.

I continued on down the hill listening to the chattering guns of the enemy planes as they attacked the marines up on the hillside. The noise of the little brook got louder and very soon I was able to scoop up the icy meltwater in my hand and drink thirstily before filling up the water bottle from the stream.

I made my way slowly back up the hill, each step I took was a supreme effort.

'Good grief, where have you been, Lofty? We thought you'd got lost or shot up.' Len said from under his steel helmet.

'No – I didn't get lost,' I said. 'But very nearly got shot up and dis-covered that it was easy enough to get downhill, but coming back up was a struggle.'

The conversation was cut short by the appearance of Sergeant Chambers.

'Keep well under cover you lot, it looks as if we are in for a rough time of it in a few moments.'

The words were hardly out of his mouth when the roar of about a dozen bombers was heard high up in the cloudless blue sky and they appeared to be heading straight for us.

The earth shook violently as the bombs struck the ground and exploded beneath it, sending up showers of rock, soil and trees.

The first wave of bombers had scarcely disappeared behind the hills when another was heard approaching and this time they were going to go for us, for they knew we were there. A stick of bombs fell above us on the hillside sending down a mixture of boulders, earth and trees. I was struck by one or two hefty rocks, one of which narrowly missed my head. So it went on until late in the afternoon when the Me 109s reappeared to repeat the machine-gunning of the two marines on the shoulder of the hill and occasionally they raked the trees where we lay sheltering from them.

It had just gone midnight on the morning of 2 May when Sergeant Chambers arrived, waking up those who were asleep and telling those who were awake to pass the word round to be ready in about ten minutes to move down to the jetty where *Sheffield* was going to try and get us off.

Admiral Leyton with two cruisers and five destroyers suffered several attacks on the way down the fjord. One destroyer was detached to collect a party that had been landed at Alesund and a second put in at Molde to take off General Ruge and other Norwegians who finally decided to follow in the wake of their King.

The rest of the rearguard force had arrived just after 11 p.m. and by midnight about 1,300 men of 15 Brigade had been taken off. After this, we made our way down through the trees towards the jetty, passing smouldering houses some of which still burned inside, visible through a curtain of smoke and dust. The time must have been about 1 p.m.

After boarding *Sheffield*, I turned and took one last look at the place where we had landed just a few days ago. No pretty houses now, only smouldering black chimney stacks standing erect like ghostly fingers. Over all a black pall of smoke that rose in the air and spilled outwards and upwards over the fjord. By 2 a.m. it was occupied by the enemy.

We were rapidly and efficiently put below decks in the *Sheffield*.

In the short time it took *Sheffield* to reach the mouth of the Romsdal fjord and the open sea, the Germans had raised the Swastika in the town of Aandalsnes.

HMS *Birmingham* was one of the last ships to leave the town. She was accompanied by the senior ships, *Manchester* and *York*. W. Brumfield, who served in the *Birmingham* tells his story of the evacuation.

> I don't remember the date exactly, but it was probably the last evacuation of British troops. The town was still burning and we could see German vehicles travelling along the coast road. I don't know what regiments our troops belonged to, but I do remember as we took them aboard that they had obviously had a rough time, very little sleep and inadequate clothing. I remember that we managed to rake up some warm underwear and socks for some of them which they greatly appreciated. I helped to serve out hot soup to them as they came aboard.
>
> There was a huge pall of thick black smoke drifting across the fjord, under which *Manchester* was sitting, thus avoiding to a great extent the odd bomb that the rest of us were getting. One of our motorboats did get hit with a bomb which did not explode but went through it into the fjord. On the way out of the fjord we saw the *York* receive a stick of bombs on either side and some of my mates swore she lifted completely out of the water.
>
> By 8 a.m. next morning, we had left Norway well behind and we could feel the throb of *Sheffield*'s mighty engines beneath our feet. Breakfast was not long in coming in the form of steaming hot soup and another doorstep of fresh ship's bread and butter.
>
> About half an hour after the meal the ship's klaxons sounded battle stations and lifeboat drill. There was almost immediate uproar. Most of us were still half asleep as we mixed in with the sailors rushing to their action

stations. On the way up to the main deck, lifebelts were thrust into our hands by other sailors and we were told to put them on. By the time we had all struggled up to the assembly station we realised it was only drill and not the real thing.

After we had been dismissed by the duty officer, two or three of us stayed behind on deck to get a breath of fresh air and have a look at the sea. We leaned on the deck rail in the shelter of a square building on the port side of the ship which housed a Walrus seaplane which *Sheffield* occasionally used for submarine spotting.

As we stood talking, the ship's tannoy crackled noisily and the voice of Bing Crosby came through singing the latest hit, 'They didn't believe me.' Suddenly, two doors swung open with a clatter on the square building amidships exposing a seaplane resting on a kind of ramp facing seawards.

We watched the pilot climb aboard with a great deal of interest and after a few more minutes, the engine burst into life with a roar. There was the usual warming up period for the benefit of the engine then the throttle-opening stage which all but deafened us. Then came a hiss as the catapult shot the Walrus bodily into the air. We watched with great interest as the submarine hunter dwindled to a speck on the horizon and finally disappeared from sight.

By the time the aircraft returned to the ship, almost half an hour had elapsed and the sky had become overcast. A rising wind began to buffet the waves, whipping the spray from the crests as it passed. We were about to go below decks when the sound of an aircraft engine became audible and we watched closely as the Walrus overtook the *Sheffield* and landed alongside in a curtain of spray. The cruiser slowed to a stop and the Walrus taxied alongside and was lifted back on board by a small jib which extended over the side of the ship.

By about 9 p.m. the same day, we passed slowly through the submarine nets at the entrance to Scapa Flow in the Orkneys and came at last to anchor in the safety of the Base.

We were the lucky ones. A lot of our comrades, the wounded and the exhausted, never even made it to Aandalsnes, but were taken prisoner by the Germans and those who did eventually get there found it a ghost town and their comrades gone. Some of them managed to dodge the Germans by escaping in various ways, even in rowing boats. Some turned back and walked over the mountains to Sweden.

But what of our comrades of 146 Brigade, codenamed Mauriceforce? This force was the complement of our own Sickleforce and was meant to be the northern pincer onto Trondheim. It consisted of three battalions of the 1/4 Lincolns, the Yorks and Lancs (Hallamshires) and the 1/4 KOYLI.

They landed at Namsos on the evening of 17 April and after advancing as far south as Steinkjer, they met the Germans advancing north and they were also attacked by the German Navy in Beitstad fjord. For 146 Brigade it was also a case of strategic withdrawals. They had no better equipment than we had but at least they had a full brigade of three battalions plus some 5,000 French forces which included the famous Chasseurs des Alpins. But they were another hundred miles nearer to the Arctic Circle and the land was not only flatter and almost treeless, but the snow was much deeper and it was much colder.

The civilian population had mostly left Namsos which was the base for 146 Brigade. After heavy bombing by the Luftwaffe, the wooden houses were very quickly destroyed, together with the railhead, rolling stock and wooden wharves.

When the destroyer *Nubian* approached the town on the night of 20 April, it was to find the whole place a mass of flames from end to end.

General Carton de Wiart VC, the Mauriceforce commander, was already speaking of the possibility that the expedition was doomed to failure. The following day, he reported to the War Office that 'Enemy aircraft have almost completely destroyed Namsos and there is little chance of carrying on any operations unless enemy air activity is considerably curtailed.'

Of course nothing of the kind happened and like ourselves in 148 Brigade, the men of Mauriceforce were left to the mercy of the Luftwaffe. Their fate was much the same as our own and by 3 May, they too were out of Norway.

Then there was Narvik. This operation was originally codenamed Rupertforce and sailed from Gourock on Friday, 12 April. It consisted of 1st Scots Guards, 1st Irish Guards and the South Wales Borderers. Subsequently reinforced by two battalions of French ski troops minus their skis and a brigade of the Foreign Legion and a Polish brigade all commanded by General Mackesy GOC 49 Division and in charge of the Narvik operations. They landed at Harstad on Monday, 15 April. Narvik, over one hundred miles inside the Arctic Circle, proved to be a more difficult problem than at first anticipated. The troops could not dig themselves in or house themselves properly. They were forced to remain outside amid rocks and snow. It was stated by critics at home that these troops were provided neither with white coats nor snow shoes and that their own clothing was inadequate for the freezing temperatures that they had to live with. There were the usual shortages, no anti-aircraft guns or field artillery and little ammunition.

By the first week in June the troops had been withdrawn from Narvik at considerable loss to the Royal Navy.

The aircraft carrier *Glorious*, sister ship to the ill-fated *Courageous*, the destroyers *Ardent* and *Acasta*, The ex-Orient liner *Arama* and the *Oilpioneer*, a tanker, all disappeared, one or two having been lost in the action of 8 June against ships that included the *Gneisenau* and the *Scharnhorst.*

The Norwegians laid down their arms at midnight on 9 June, thus ending the storm that had swept over the mountains and fjords of Norway.

In the unpublished memoirs of the late Chief Petty Officer Jack T. Briggs, Leading Telegraphist RN, he says he went to war with a bacon butty in his hand and his kit left behind on a jetty, to take part in one of Britain's military disasters to be shortly carried out in the sub-Arctic wastes of Norway.

Jack was a bridegroom of just seven days when he took that fateful trip with his bacon butty to board HMS *Pelican* only to find that the radio gear that he needed was in her sister ship *Black Swan.*

Since October 1939 the Allies as well as the Germans had been concerned about the extensive iron ore exports from Sweden that the Germans especially needed, and which the Allies were determined to put a stop to. And the Swedes were very fearful that if they stopped supplies they too would be invaded.

Finally, plans emerged in 1940 aimed at assisting the Finns against the invading Russians, and by occupying northern Norway, to deny Swedish ore to the Germans. This was Plan 4.

In 1939 these plans were as yet unknown to Lt William Donald, then standing by the sloop *Black Swan,* or to Leading Telegraphist Jack Briggs in HMS *Malaya,* or to Able Seaman John patrolling in HMS *Wanderer,* to

Cruiser HMS *Sheffield.*

Able Seaman Aubrey Challis in HMS *Barham* and Bill Black, Basil Tammans, Sam Snudden, Eric Shepherd and Boy 1st Class Bob Shepherd in HMS *Nelson*, or to hundreds of men in the Leicester and Nottingham areas only recently called up. Christmas came and *Nelson* was undergoing some repairs in Portsmouth Dockyard with some hundred Royal Marines and sixty seamen on board who had been earmarked for Plan 4.

After the war, Jack Briggs wanted to piece together the fate of the crew of the Chatham-based sloop, HMS *Pelican* and the Royal Marines who were put ashore at Aandalsnes, along with the poorly equipped and totally inexperienced Territorial Army battalions.

HMS *Cairo*, an anti-aircraft defence cruiser, was another vessel manned by a Chatham crew. Together, with other ships they comprised Operation Primrose, which turned into such a deadly fiasco that the real story became a top secret lest it damage British morale in 1940 when the nation had to face up to yet another disaster within a matter of days – that of Dunkirk. Briggs said:

> The Chatham survivors, if any, would be a vital link in this 'unheralded disaster' which saw the lads from the TA pass like ghosts in the night, most to their deaths and others to spend the long stretch of the war in some remote prison camp in eastern Europe.

It was on 13 April that the decision was taken by the Admiralty that an extra force would be provided from whatever and wherever. That was when Lieutenant William Donald and those others previously mentioned, suddenly and without notice, training or outfitting, became involved. From *Barham*, *Nelson* and *Hood*, together with small contingents of Royal Marines from other ships in harbour, about 700 men, trained (?) but not suitably equipped, were standing to. At the last minute *Barham* substituted 30 seamen for the Marines. From the barracks, HMS *Victory*, a small party of wireless and signal ratings were taken off normal promotion courses and given an acquaintance course on Iceland and Reykjavik in particular. They were piled onto a train in the barracks siding at 6 a.m. on Sunday, 14 April, together with the ratings from ships in harbour and were on their way to Rosyth. No arrangements had been made to provide food for the journey and being Sunday no civilian resources were available either. The Salvation Army provided cups of tea at York. The petty officer in charge was unable to get any food, or promise of food. Their thirst a little assuaged by the tea, the sailors slept as best they could and eventually the train arrived alongside some ships in Rosyth Dockyard between 9.30 and 10 p.m. It was cold and it was raining.

*   *   *

In the Signals Section of the Military Training College at Catterick 2nd Lieutenant Butler was imbibing the full implications of setting up a field station at Aandalsnes to communicate with the army radio station near Catterick. Apparently, the most essential element of this attempt to provide a reliable link was to be a high gain directional rhomboid antenna, which would require siting on an accurate bearing aimed at Catterick. This, Mr Butler explained to the senior W/T rating soon after he had landed on the Norwegian coast, would therefore preclude any hope of a regular schedule between his station at Catterick and the naval station about to be established at Aandalsnes. The senior rating expressed his opinion that in the light of the persistent bombing by the Luftwaffe, a bit of barbed wire might be more suitable and much less conspicuous.

The army failed to establish a reliable link with Catterick, but this is jumping the gun by about four days.

On 15 April, *Black Swan, Flamingo, Bittern* and *Auckland* slipped out of harbour and sped at high speed (10 knots) across the North Sea. William Donald and William Black have both described the approach, but Bill Black was close to the action and wrote:

> Moving up the fjord, everything seemed silent except for the throbbing of the ship's engines. Once alongside at Aandalsnes things went like clock-work. *Flamingo* wanted to get back down the fjord and out to sea. We got into billets up the road, to wait for orders before moving up. Meantime some were guarding officers' quarters, installations, etc.; myself among others, were moving ammo from the dockside to a dump which I thought to be on the Dombaas road.
>
> Then came the big push, objective Stavanger Airfield. The Germans came down by parachute. Some had fold-up bikes, all had semi-automatic weapons. Our one and only howitzer, with limber, had become a bit of a health hazard by this time; we lost it down a hillside. Just as well, for the necessary ammunition landed from *Black Swan* was 4 in instead of the required 3.7 in.

George Watson, another seaman from *Nelson*, is a little less certain of events leading up to the landings, except that the howitzer figured largely, and was a problem. He also was part of the field gun crew. George recalls that there were two battalions landed by the army, the 1/5th Leicesters and the 1/8th Sherwood Foresters. They were all hurried onto trains headed for the front beyond Dombaas.

> Bill Black and another seaman were detailed to guard a wireless station that had been set up a couple of miles out of town. They were not to approach the station and they were to ensure that no one else did either.

After two days with no sign of life therein they did approach and found the station deserted and the equipment damaged by blast. As the naval W/T station was transferred to Molde 24 hours after the arrival of Lt Butler and was transferred intact, it must be assumed that they had been guarding the army station. Anyway Bill and the other seaman smashed up what was left and reported back to base.

The transfer of the naval W/T station took place on 20 April after consultation with the Army HQ. The general opinion was that the army would be able to establish its wireless links and it was desirable that the navy provided the back up from Molde where the port facilities were more extensive and obviated the long passage up the Romsdal fjord; three to four hours steaming at 15 knots, the best speed that most merchant navy vessels could achieve.

The passage in a small Norwegian coaster was uneventful. The needs for weaponry had been solved in that the party of seven had been armed with rifles and the Leading rates also had 24 rounds of 0.45 in. for the Webley pistols provided. Additionally, there was a Lewis gun, discarded by the Marines. There was no other army or naval personnel involved. We were very patently on our own. Rations were also provided in the form of a case of issue biscuits.

The arrival at Molde was almost a celebration, units of Sickleforce had passed through and pressed on to Aandalsnes and beyond. The wireless was installed adjacent to a nearby garage.

Shortly after 10 a.m. two Heinkels appeared, had a good look around at about 4,000 feet, sprinkled some incendiaries near the jetties and left. Shortly after 3 p.m. a larger sortie of bombers arrived.

A second transmitter receiver outfit had been delivered and was kept in a warehouse near the hotel. Also there was now a day and night frequency plan which enabled the crew to set up the two stations at some distance apart. Of the crew that should have accompanied this and more powerful equipment, there was no sign, although it was confirmed that the chief petty officer had been severely wounded when a bomb hit the stern of HMS *Pelican*. This left the original four wireless ratings to carry on. Things were getting a little on the messy side by 25 April. The whole of Molde was virtually destroyed. The intensity of enemy bombing had increased and it became necessary to find a new location during daylight hours and move the equipment under cover of the hour or two of semi-darkness which came in the early hours. When the move was complete a few dots and dashes on the key told the live station to close down and get some sleep until another location had been found.

There was only one bad moment when a bomb fell just outside the cellar where the W/T was operating and failed to explode. The biggest problem was maintaining petrol supplies for the generator. It was too heavy to move around, so they had to find and carry fuel when and how they could. At one time it was a mixture of aviation spirit and paraffin found in a dump outside the town. Two of rum and one of water was a fair guideline for the mixture. As the signal traffic was all in code, they had to rely on the visits of the dispatch riders to keep them up to date with the situation. Except for HMS *Glasgow* which arrived in a shower of fire mains and left with the Crown and its jewels, they knew not who they were. As soon as it was alongside they returned to their nightly task of moving home again.

About two nights after *Glasgow* left we were told that if there were no ships to take us off within the next 24 hours we would be free to make our own way out.

We were still operating with what I suspect were dummy messages to maintain the fiction that we were still there in force. Thankfully, the *Ulster Princess* appeared out of the gloom and carried us to Scapa Flow.

Back in the Romsdal valley George Watson recalls that the German raids were fairly regular at four hourly intervals between 8 a.m. and 6 p.m. Most raids lasted for about an hour, so when the order was given to get out, they found that there were very few boats and the jetties were so damaged that no ship could get alongside. As they watched men trying to get to a destroyer, some even swimming and failing, he and Bill Black decided that it would be better to walk. With two others of the crew and three RAF, they set out on a flatbed lorry. There were a few army and some civilians but a few miles out of Aandalsnes a Dornier came gliding down towards them with his engines cut. They slipped off the truck and into a ditch. The Dornier did not open fire. From now on it was foot slogging all the way, keeping clear of the open road until it was too dark when they bedded down on a hillside. The next day, they pushed on until they reached a place called Hen where they were caught in open ground. A couple of aircraft strafed them but luckily no one was hit. Bill was stuck in a snowdrift up to his waist. Further on, the road became a narrow trail and then they saw a large barnlike building with a road barrier across the trail. This meant another detour for a couple of miles until they could get back to a decent road. Ahead, lay the only bridge between them and Molde. From here they could look back along the fjord and see the way they had come. They travelled in semi-darkness as the road was better and no aircraft to interrupt their journey. Hugging the coastline, they no longer cared about the Bosch, they were just looking for any way to get out of Norway. Coming up to some partly demolished buildings they met a stocky major who looked a bit on the old side. Still, anyone who was there would expect to look old whatever his age. There was a group of army personnel sheltering in the ruins, some on stretchers. Asked by the major what Bill thought were their chances of getting away, Bill looked at the blokes and thought the poor buggers need a boost, so he told the major that they could be pretty good. As Bill said in his letter to me, his thoughts were 'Oh God, please let it be true. These boys look as if they have roughed it too long.'

Meantime, three of the matelots set off to beg food and drink from the surrounding houses. The first reaction was; not on, they probably had little enough for themselves, but at the third try they were lucky. These folks gave them a can of goat's milk and a basket of muffins, to share out. Bill regrets that he didn't have time to return the basket as out in the fjord they saw some ships and he recognised the 'woodbine' funnel as that of *Wanderer*, which quickly pulled alongside and dropped her scrambling nets. Bill told the major to get his men going and they made their way up the nets onto the ship. No sooner were they aboard than she ran aground as she turned away. Boats were lowered to transfer them to the *Southampton* until they were clear, and finally to the *Ulster Monarch* and then to somewhere in Scotland.

It has not been possible to obtain any first-hand reports of the part the Royal Marines played in the operations in Norway. The official line as published in the history of the Royal Marines shows that a force of 250 occupied the Faeroes on 13 April and over 700 marines and seamen landed to secure the railhead at Aandalsnes on 17 April, followed by Sickleforce on 18th.

On 12 April the Adjutant General, General Bourne, who had been studying maps of the Central Norway arena, received permission to land a force of Marines at Aandalsnes to hold the port until the army arrived. The force was drawn mainly from three warships undergoing repair, The *Hood, Nelson* and *Barham*, the 21st LAA battery Royal Marines and the 11th Searchlight Regiment. However Lt Col H.W. Simpson soon found that there was no room for all the troops on the four sloops detailed to transport the force which had been designated Operation Primrose to Norway. Later Simpson stated that a few hours' delay in sailing would have been justified to allow a reasonable plan for loading the sloops. As it was, they were so heavily loaded that they were drawing over a foot more than their normal draught. The stores on deck included 4-in coastal guns and eight 2-pounder pompoms. These last mentioned were incomplete with pieces of string in place of the wires for their 'spider web' gunsights; the coast guns were also found to be incomplete. The force had been assembled and was at sea within 72 hours of receiving first orders. Such haste was to prove disastrous in the end. As the sloops made their way at their best speed in the heavy weather – about ten knots – Colonel Simpson's orders were altered and amended several times, but finally settled on Aandalsnes at 10 p.m. on Wednesday 17 April. (This contradicts other reports which place the landings 24 hours earlier – but the hour stated here is correct.) Each sloop was unloaded in turn, the whole operation taking nine hours. (Here again the recollections of the actual landing parties differ in that the unloading was completed within six hours, but a further nine hours were spent clearing the jetty.)

Air attacks did not occur on the first day of the landings, due largely to the bombardment of the seaplane base and the aerodrome at Stavanger by HMS *Suffolk* and four destroyers. *Flamingo* was bombed as the crew sat down to lunch. (See William Donald's 'Stand by for Action'.) *Suffolk* had to abandon the attack at 6 a.m. as the sunlight was too bright to observe the flashes of her shells exploding. Also the radio of her 'fall of shot' spotting Walrus was not working.

Suffolk withdrew and about two hours later, the first of thirty air attacks began. They lasted until mid-afternoon X and Y turrets were put out of action, but *Suffolk* reached Scapa Flow with her decks awash. Eighteen marines had been killed and fifteen wounded.

Meanwhile Colonel Simpson had found that he was without any maps of the area and the roads could only be kept open with snowploughs and to bring stores and munitions from Molde, the other landing point, the transport had to cross by ferries and some 80 km of roadway.

The following day, 148 Brigade landed with orders to attack northwards from Dombaas some 110 km further south, but 200 of the marines had already left for Dombaas to hold the German paras that were occupying the heights overlooking the town and the railway.

Of these exploits a sergeant engaged in transport in the area said 'German bombers raided every day from 7 a.m. to 5 p.m. There was never a break in the attacks. I never thought that Germany possessed so many bombs. At Aandalsnes they dropped at least a thousand in a couple of days. On the day we left, the only part of the town they had missed was the concrete jetty. All the main parts of the jetty were of wood and had vanished very early in the campaign.'

The other landings at Namsos by 146 Brigade which were to form the northern part of the pincer movement to capture Trondheim were equally disastrous and bedevilled by the same lack of decisiveness on the part of the military and political heads back in England. It must be said that there was a complete misunderstanding of the problems involved in maintaining a reliable and efficient communications link between the forces in the field and the remote Norwegian headquarters. The navy had more than adequate communicators, both visual and radio, but was deficient in coping with the heavily increased load of 'encyphered' traffic. The idea that the Surgeon with officers off watch could cope with such traffic proved to be inept. Also it is questionable that much of the traffic merited the high degree of security inherent in grading operational traffic at 'Officers Only' level. By 1941, this had been rectified by the formation of the Ratings Coder branch and a relaxation of the requirement to decode all traffic intercepted. A further improvement was to institute a series of 'Dangerous Waters' code books, all others being landed or destroyed before entering on similar operations in the future. The basic fault was that even if they wished to do so, there was no easy way for the various arms of the forces involved to talk to each other. Even without encoding signals. On-line scramblers were not available for general use.

I have been able to gain little first-hand information in this field of the experiences of the army units involved and have to rely on abstracts from various official records of various nationalities for what is said to have occurred. Certainly there are reports of disagreements, of orders by generals and admirals which were not compatible and 'in extremis', decisions by commanders in the field to ignore directives from Whitehall and cooperate with the local Norwegian commanders. Of the men themselves, there is little doubt that they gave more than should have been expected of them and those who were lucky enough to get away returned home very disillusioned. An appreciable number found their way home in small vessels, without proper navigational aids or skills, others by escape over the mountains to Sweden or eventually as returned prisoners after the war. But there is no guidance that I have been able to find that enables one to put a figure on those who lived to tell the tale.

Of the RAF contingent, it should suffice to say that when the eighteen Gloster Gladiators from the aircraft carrier *Glorious* landed on the frozen Lake Lesjaskog some twenty miles north west of Dombaas, they found that the fuel that was destined for them had been landed at Molde, where it remained until after the departure of the Norwegian monarchy and High Command in HMS *Glasgow* together with the country's gold reserves. Although about thirty RAF personnel were on their way to Molde from Aandalsnes on 30 April, they had not arrived by 10 p.m. on 3 May.

This story would not be complete without a mention of the two Liverpool–Belfast ferry boats, the *Ulster Monarch* and the *Ulster Princess,* built for fast passenger traffic between the Mersey and Northern Ireland. Unarmed and undegaussed, without escort or air cover, they steamed around the Romsdal fjord picking up odd groups of survivors, taking the first pickups to the Shetlands and then returning to Aandalsnes and Molde on 2/3 May to take off the very last to come away from the area. The *Monarch* went to the Clyde with her last load and the *Princess* to Scapa Flow.

It may seem that this aspect of the Central Norwegian affair has been heavily biased towards the naval with little input from the Royal Marines or the army units involved. Despite appeals to various authorities it has not been possible to locate a single representative of the Royal Marines who was actually present at either Aandalsnes or Dombaas. It has been stated that the majority were evacuated, but very few of those who were serving in *Nelson* returned to the ship after the evacuation. Those who were serving in *Hood* and *Barham*, like many of their naval counterparts, were still serving in these ships when they were sunk in the Atlantic or Mediterranean. At least it has been confirmed that this was true in the case of *Barham*; although the source for this statement had left *Barham* before she went to Alexandria, he confirmed that the ship's company was substantially the same as was carried in April 1940. Here also, only a few returned to the ship from Norway.

The total loss of the ship's company in *Hood* means that there has been no feedback from this vessel. There is no doubt that those of the light ack-ack and searchlight units returned safely as they were deployed adjacent to but away from Aandalsnes, and, with the lack of effective weaponry, did not invite the attention of the Luftwaffe.

It was on the 27th according to Bill Hinton, who was the A/S petty officer and was on the bridge with Captain Poland, that *Black Swan* expended over two thousand rounds of 4 in and some 4,000 rounds of pompom, which was the entire supply for the whole navy forecast for the next week and up to mid-May.

General Paget had now been appointed to command this improvised and diversionary attack by 15 Brigade and which appeared to be escalating into a general invasion. He arrived 24 hours after his brigade to learn that the War Council had decided to evacuate all the forces in the Romsdal and Namsos areas by 1 May. Although many of the late arrivals managed to embark at Aandalsnes, both the remnants of Primrose and Sickleforce had to find their way down the north side of the fjord in the direction of Molde. Few of them reached Molde to be taken off by destroyers. In these operations, HMS *Wanderer* and *Imperial* played a major part.

This then, is my story and my gratitude is extended to all those who helped me put it together, especially the media who put me in contact with comrades who enabled some of the jigsaw pieces to fit together to remember those who strayed into the Home of the Giants and stayed behind in the Cradle of Freedom forever.

Upon our arrival in Scapa Flow, we, the remnants of the 1/5th Battalion of the Leicesters, were transferred from *Sheffield* to *Rodney* and after spending the night on board, we were transferred the following day to the Polish liner *Gdynia Sobieski*.

We took part in some of the shipboard duties like fire piquet and sentry duty and occasionally there would be a boat drill.

We arrived in Glasgow on 6 May, where we were issued with new kit. Here we were addressed at length by the CIGS General Ironside, who, amongst other things told us:

'You were in no sense driven out of Norway. You were ordered out.'

Private Joseph H. Kynoch, aged 22 in 1941, in dress uniform of the Royal Army Ordnance Corps, later the Royal Electrical and Mechanical Engineers.

Cassandra, writing in the *Daily Mirror* the following day, quickly picked this up and asked the question in his column 'Who by – the Germans?'

On Saturday, 18 May, the Mayor of Loughborough gave a civic reception for the local lads from the town and whilst we were on leave the German invasion of the Netherlands had begun.

We went back from leave refreshed to rejoin our battalion at Portobello, Edinburgh. Here we remained for several weeks to rebuild our depleted forces. We were not only brought up to strength again but we were issued with brand new transport and equipment.

Early in July, we moved as a battalion to Stranraer on the west coast of Scotland and thence sailed across to Larne, and finally to the little village of Caledon on the Irish border, where we settled for the rest of that year.

Early in January 1941 I found I had been selected to go on a basic engineering course at a technical college in Walthamstow, London.

By June 1941, I had finished my training and was transferred to the REME in which I served for the rest of the war, finishing with the 14th Army in South East Asia. But that is another story which I am at present working on.

EPILOGUE

Looking back in hindsight after more than sixty years, there is very little to add to what has already been written about the political and military blunders which were the direct cause of the fiasco of the Norwegian campaign and which was quickly followed by the much bigger shambles of Dunkirk.

During the thirties we all knew what Hitler and Mussolini were up to, yet our politicians sat and watched them rise to power and march into first one country and then another. They were too preoccupied with winning the next election.

How could these men sit and do nothing from 1935 when the Italians attacked Abyssinia through the Spanish civil war in 1936 instigated by the Fascists and finally to the declaration of war on Germany for attacking Poland in September 1939? They knew full well that the gun room was empty and the RAF depended on weekend flyers in a handful of un-warlike planes.

There was little cohesion with French pre-war policy since they changed their governments almost every six months. Their old generals

Corporal Arthur Thomas,
C Coy Leicesters.

from the First World War were called out of retirement to help stem the advance of the Germans but to no avail. It was all too late and the 'old' generals couldn't cope with the swiftly moving armour, the swarms of aircraft, the fifth columnists and the confusion they spread.

In a week or so after we got back home, the allied armies in France were having a taste of what we had to contend with in Norway; on a larger scale but in fine and warm sunny weather. Like us, they couldn't stop the advance of the Germans and so came the evacuation of Dunkirk.

But how do we remember the men who fell in the battle for Norway? For almost fifty years, the headstone over the grave of a British soldier lying in the cemetery of a church in the little town of Lillehammer carried the simple epitaph 'A soldier of the Second World War, 21st April, 1940. Known only unto God'. The identity of the soldier, who died helping his comrades to defend the town against the advancing German army, was discovered by an officer of the Royal Marines, Major Ian Binnie in 1988. With the help of Mr Per Aspesletten of Lillehammer, he started an investigation into the identity of the 'Unknown Soldier'.

An entry in the parish church register showed that the man was a

Lillehammer station in 1990. H.D. Murfet and Tom Wortley, veterans of the Leicesters.

Joseph Kynoch, Kjell Elvestad, local photographer and Lt Col Eilert Overland at Lillehammer in 1999.

Joseph Kynoch and Kjell Elvestad on Tretten bridge in 1999.

Privates Jim 'Nuffy' Hall, Archie Pratt and L/Cpl Bindley, all of MT
Platoon, Leicesters.

Sherwood Forester of the 1/8th Battalion killed on 21 April 1940. The
Norwegian records also showed that the soldier was wearing a ring
engraved with the words 'To Frank from Marion' and with the initials
F.G.

On his return to England, the marine officer contacted the secretary of
the regiment and they searched the archives; eventually, it was discovered that the soldier was Private Frank Godwin, who was reported
'missing in action' in April 1940. The records showed that he was killed
on his thirtieth birthday.

It does not take much to imagine what the feelings of his family must
have been over those years not knowing what had happened to their
loved one. The mystery could have been solved soon after the event with
some effort by the War Office, but he was just a number, and having
given his life as a soldier, he had fulfilled his requirements and that was
that.

There are very few of us left now of 148 Brigade who were able to go

164

An Aerial view of Kvam.

Memorial to British soldiers in Lillehammer Cemetery.

165

to the ceremony at Lillehammer on 17 May 1989 to erect a new head-stone over Frank Godwin's grave, to coincide with Norway's National Day celebrations. Most of us were in our seventies and some were too infirm to go. If only something had been organised earlier. It is a great pity that the inhumanity of the system has enabled the whole campaign to remain forgotten, along with those who fought in it. The Norwegians have done a lot more for the fallen of that ill-fated expedition. I have seen how tidy they keep the graves of the British fallen, with flowers in season in the little village churches in the Gudbrandsdal valley of Norway.

GLOSSARY

2IC	Second in Command
ADS	Active Duty Support
BEF	British Expeditionary Force
BTO	Battalion Transport Officer
CIGS	Chief of the Imperial General Staff
CPO	Chief Petty Officer
CQMS	Company Quartermaster Sergeant
CSM	Company Sergeant Major
IO	Intelligence Officer
KOYLI	King's Own Yorkshire Light Infantry
LAA	Light Anti-Aircraft Artillery
MO	Medical Officer
MT	Motor Transport
NCO	Non-commissioned Officer
PSM	Platoon Sergeant Major
QM	Quartermaster
RE	Royal Engineers
REME	Royal Electrical and Mechanical Engineers
RQMS	Regimental Quartermaster Sergeant
RSM	Regimental Sergeant Major
W/T	Wireless Telegraphist

BIBLIOGRAPHY

The People's History of World War 2
Odhams Press

The unpublished diary of the Campaign in Norway
Captain E.C.G. Beckwith 1/8th Sherwood Foresters

The History of the Royal Leicestershire Regiment

The Imperial War Museum

Other Comrades' experiences

Stand by for Action: Donald, W.

INDEX

Page numbers in *italics* refer to illustrations.